# Overcoming Past Pain

Dealing with Toxic People, Verbally Abusive Relationships,
Empower Yourself, Overcome Trauma

Cathleen R. Barton

I0619904

Overcoming Past Pain: Dealing with Toxic People, Verbally Abusive Relationships, Empower Yourself, Overcome Trauma

# Table of Contents

# Book 1 - Dealing with Toxic People

Understanding and Managing the Negative Impact of Difficult Individuals in Your Personal and Professional Life, and Strategies for Protecting Your Emotional and Mental Well-being

# 01: Understanding the Different Types of Toxic People

Toxic people come in many forms, and it can be difficult to recognize and deal with them in our daily lives. Understanding the different types of toxic individuals can help us to better protect ourselves from their negative influence and improve our overall well-being.

One of the most common types of toxic people is the narcissist. Narcissists are characterized by their extreme self-absorption and lack of empathy for others. They often manipulate and exploit those around them for their own gain, and have little regard for the feelings or needs of others. They may also engage in gaslighting, a form of manipulation that involves making others doubt their own reality or memories.

Another type of toxic individual is the manipulator. Manipulators use deceit and manipulation to control and exploit those around them. They may use tactics such as lying, guilt-tripping, and playing the victim in order to get what they want. They often lack empathy and may be skilled at making others feel guilty or ashamed for not giving in to their demands.

# 01: UNDERSTANDING THE DIFFERENT TYPES OF TOXIC PEOPLE

The passive-aggressive individual is another type of toxic person. Passive-aggressive individuals may seem friendly and cooperative on the surface, but they often use subtle forms of aggression to express their dissatisfaction or anger. They may make snide or sarcastic comments, or engage in subtle forms of sabotage in order to get their way. They are often difficult to confront or call out, as their behavior may be hard to pin down.

Another common type of toxic individual is the controller. Controllers are often obsessed with power and control, and will go to great lengths to assert their dominance over others. They may be domineering, demanding, and possessive in their relationships, and may use verbal or physical abuse to maintain control. They may also use manipulation and gaslighting to make others doubt themselves or their own reality.

The victim mentality is also a form of toxicity, this type of individual tends to play the role of the victim in order to gain sympathy and attention. They may exaggerate their problems or difficulties, or blame others for their misfortune. They tend to be emotionally unstable, and may be difficult to help or support due to their constant complaints and refusal to take responsibility for their own actions.

It's important to note that not all toxic people fit neatly into these categories, and some individuals may exhibit traits of more than one type. Additionally, not everyone who exhibits toxic behavior is doing so intentionally. Some people may be unaware of their own negative impact on others, and may need help to change their behavior.

In any case, dealing with toxic people can be challenging, but it is possible to protect yourself from their negative influence. One of the most important things you can do is to set and maintain healthy boundaries. This means communicating clearly and assertively about what you will and will not tolerate from others, and sticking to those boundaries even when it's uncomfortable.

It's also important to take care of yourself, both physically and emotionally. This may involve seeking support from friends and family, practicing self-care, and seeking professional help if necessary. Keeping a journal or talking to a therapist can also be helpful in dealing with the emotional fallout from toxic relationships.

## 01: UNDERSTANDING THE DIFFERENT TYPES OF TOXIC PEOPLE

Ultimately, understanding the different types of toxic people can help us to better recognize and deal with them in our lives. By setting healthy boundaries, taking care of ourselves, and seeking support when necessary, we can protect ourselves from their negative influence and improve our overall well-being.

Another important aspect of dealing with toxic people is learning to recognize the warning signs of toxic behavior. Some common indicators include:

– Constant criticism and negative comments

– Attempts to control or manipulate others

– Lack of empathy or concern for others

– Refusal to take responsibility for their actions

– Constant complaints and negative attitude

When you notice these warning signs in someone you know, it's important to take steps to protect yourself. This may involve limiting your contact with them, setting boundaries, or even ending the relationship altogether. It's important to remember that you have the right to choose the people you surround yourself with, and you don't have to continue to be in a relationship with someone who is harmful to you.

It's also important to remember that toxic people can come in many forms, and they may not always be easy to spot. Sometimes, toxic individuals may be disguised as friends, family members, or even romantic partners. It's important to be vigilant and trust your instincts when you sense that someone may be toxic.

When it comes to dealing with toxic people, there are a few strategies that may be helpful:

– Establish clear boundaries. Communicate your needs and limits clearly, and don't be afraid to assert yourself if someone is crossing your boundaries.

– Learn to say "no." It's important to be able to say "no" when someone is asking for something that you're not com-fortable with or that would be harmful to you.

– Set limits on your time and energy. Limit the amount of time you spend with toxic people, and don't hesitate to take a break from them if necessary.

– Seek support. Surround yourself with positive, supportive people, and don't be afraid to seek professional help if necessary.

– Practice self-care. Take care of yourself both physically and emotionally, and make sure you're getting enough rest and exercise.

It's important to remember that dealing with toxic people can be difficult and draining, and it's important to take care of yourself during this process. Sometimes, the best thing you can do is to simply remove yourself from the situation and surround yourself with positive, supportive people.

In conclusion, toxic people come in many forms and can have a negative impact on our lives. By understanding the different types of toxic individuals, recognizing the warning signs of toxic behavior, and implementing strategies to protect ourselves, we can improve our overall well-being and live a healthier, happier life. Remember to set boundaries, practice self-care, and seek support when necessary.

# 02: The Impact of Toxic People on Your Emotional and Mental Well-being

Toxic people can have a significant negative impact on one's emotional and mental well-being. These individuals can be found in all areas of life, including in the home, at work, and in social circles. They can be family members, friends, coworkers, or even strangers. Their toxic behavior can take many forms, such as verbal abuse, manipulation, and neglect.

The effects of toxic people on emotional and mental well-being can be devastating. These individuals can cause feelings of anxiety, depression, and self-doubt. They can also contribute to the development of negative self-talk and a lack of self-worth.

One of the most damaging effects of toxic people is their ability to manipulate others. They often use tactics such as gaslighting, in which they make their victims question their own sanity and reality. They may also use guilt and shame as a means of control. These tactics can leave individuals feeling confused, paranoid, and isolated.

## 02: THE IMPACT OF TOXIC PEOPLE ON YOUR EMOTIONAL AND MENTAL WELL-BEING

Toxic people can also contribute to the development of unhealthy coping mechanisms, such as substance abuse and self-harm. They can also make it difficult for an individual to form healthy relationships in the future.

The key to protecting oneself from the negative effects of toxic people is to recognize their behavior and set boundaries. This means learning to say "no" and standing up for oneself. It also means learning to recognize the warning signs of toxic behavior and avoiding those individuals.

It's also important to surround oneself with supportive and healthy individuals. This can include friends, family, and professionals such as therapists or counselors. These individuals can provide a sounding board for one's thoughts and feelings, and can offer guidance and support.

It's also important to practice self-care and self-compassion. This includes engaging in activities that bring joy and relaxation, such as exercise, reading, and spending time with loved ones. It also means being kind to oneself and practicing self-compassion.

In summary, toxic people can have a significant negative

impact on one's emotional and mental well-being. Their behavior can cause feelings of anxiety, depression, self-doubt, and can contribute to the development of unhealthy coping mechanisms. To protect oneself, it's important to recognize toxic behavior and set boundaries, surround oneself with supportive individuals, and practice self-care and self-compassion.

It's important to remember that toxic people often have their own issues and struggles that contribute to their behavior. It's not always easy, but try to have compassion for the person and understand that their actions are not a reflection of your worth as a person.

It's also important to address toxic behavior in a constructive manner. This means being clear and direct about what is not acceptable and what the consequences of that behavior will be. It's also important to be open to feedback and willing to listen to the other person's perspective.

However, sometimes it is necessary to remove toxic people from your life completely. This can be a difficult decision, but it may be necessary for your own emotional and mental well-being. It's important to remember that your safety and well-being should be the top priority.

It's also important to seek professional help if you find yourself struggling with the effects of toxic people in your life. A therapist or counselor can provide support and guidance as you navigate the healing process. They can also provide tools and strategies for dealing with toxic individuals and building healthier relationships in the future.

In conclusion, toxic people can have a significant negative impact on one's emotional and mental well-being. However, by recognizing toxic behavior, setting boundaries, surrounding oneself with supportive individuals, practicing self-care and self-compassion, and seeking professional help, it is possible to protect oneself from the negative effects of toxic people. Remember to take care of yourself, and don't hesitate to reach out for help if you need it.

# 03: Recognizing the Signs of a Toxic Relationship

A toxic relationship can be defined as any relationship in which one or both parties experience negative and harmful effects, such as emotional abuse, manipulation, and control. These relationships can be incredibly damaging and can have lasting effects on a person's mental and physical health. It is important to be able to recognize the signs of a toxic relationship so that you can take steps to get out of one before it becomes too harmful.

One of the most common signs of a toxic relationship is a feeling of constant negativity. If you feel like your partner is always criticizing you, belittling you, or making you feel bad about yourself, this is a sign that the relationship is toxic. Additionally, if your partner is always angry, jealous, or possessive, this can also indicate that the relationship is unhealthy.

Another sign of a toxic relationship is a lack of trust and communication. If your partner is always checking up on you, monitoring your phone or social media, or making you feel like you can't be yourself, this is a sign that the relationship is not healthy. Additionally, if your partner is always lying to you or hiding things from you, this can also indicate that the relationship is toxic.

Another common sign of a toxic relationship is control and manipulation. If your partner is always trying to control what you do, who you talk to, or what you wear, this is a sign that the relationship is toxic. Additionally, if your partner is always trying to manipulate you into doing things that you don't want to do, this is also a sign that the relationship is unhealthy.

Another sign of a toxic relationship is physical or emotional abuse. Physical abuse includes any kind of physical violence, such as hitting, pushing, or restraining. Emotional abuse includes any kind of psychological manipulation, such as gaslighting, intimidation, or manipulation. If your partner is physically or emotionally abusive, it is important to get out of the relationship as soon as possible.

It is important to note that these signs may not be present in all toxic relationships, and that toxic relationships can take on many different forms. However, if you are experiencing any of the above signs in your relationship, it is important to take steps to get out of the relationship as soon as possible.

There are many different ways to exit a toxic relationship, including seeking help from a therapist or counselor, seeking help from a domestic violence shelter or hotline, and talking to trusted friends or family members. It is also important to have a safety plan in place in case your partner becomes violent or threatening.

Ultimately, it is important to remember that you deserve to be in a healthy and loving relationship, and that you should never stay in a relationship that is harmful to your mental or physical well-being. Recognizing the signs of a toxic relationship is the first step in taking control of your life and finding the happiness and fulfillment that you deserve.

It is important to remember that leaving a toxic relationship can be hard, and it may take some time to heal. But with the right support and resources, it is possible to move on and find a healthy and fulfilling relationship. Remember that you are not alone and that there are people who can help you navigate this difficult time.

It's also important to understand that toxic relationships often involve a cycle of abuse, where the abuser may apologize and promise to change, only to repeat the same harmful behavior again. This is known as the "cycle of abuse," and it can be difficult to break out of. The abuser may also use various tactics, such as gaslighting, to make the victim question their own reality and doubt their own perceptions.

It's important to remember that leaving a toxic relationship is not a sign of weakness, but of strength and courage. It's important to take care of yourself, both physically and emotionally, during this time. It's also important to have a support system in place, whether it's friends, family, or a therapist.

It's also important to understand that healing from a toxic relationship takes time and patience. It's important to give yourself time to process your feelings and emotions, and to not blame yourself for what happened. It's also important to understand that it may take some time to regain trust in others and to develop healthy relationships in the future.

It's also important to understand that it's not only romantic relationships that can be toxic. Friendship, familial relationships, and even work relationships can also be toxic. It's important to be aware of the signs and to take steps to remove yourself from these types of relationships as well.

It's also important to remember that it's possible to have a healthy relationship in the future. It's important to learn from past experiences and to seek out healthy relationships in the future. It's also important to be aware of the signs of a toxic relationship and to set boundaries for yourself in future relationships.

In conclusion, recognizing the signs of a toxic relationship is important in order to take steps to get out of one before it becomes too harmful. The signs of a toxic relationship can include constant negativity, a lack of trust and communication, control and manipulation, and physical or emotional abuse. It's important to have a support system in place, to take care of yourself, and to understand that healing takes time and patience. Remember that you deserve to be in a healthy and loving relationship, and don't hesitate to seek help if you need it.

# 04: Setting Healthy Boundaries with Difficult Individuals

Setting healthy boundaries with difficult individuals is an important aspect of self-care and maintaining healthy relationships. It can be challenging to navigate interactions with people who are demanding, controlling, or otherwise challenging to be around. However, by learning to set clear and assertive boundaries, you can take control of your own well-being and improve your relationships with others.

One of the first steps in setting healthy boundaries with difficult individuals is to understand the difference between healthy and unhealthy boundaries. Healthy boundaries are those that protect your physical, emotional, and mental well-being. They allow you to have a sense of self and to make your own choices without feeling guilty or pressured. Unhealthy boundaries, on the other hand, are those that are too rigid or too lax, and they can lead to feelings of resentment, guilt, or being taken advantage of.

Once you understand the difference between healthy and unhealthy boundaries, you can start to set them with difficult individuals. This may involve setting limits on what you are willing to tolerate in terms of behavior or communication, as well as setting clear expectations for how you want to be treated. For example, if a difficult individual is constantly demanding your time and attention, you may need to set a boundary by setting aside specific times when you are available to interact with them. You can also set boundaries by saying "no" to requests or demands that are unreasonable or that make you feel uncomfortable.

It's important to remember that setting boundaries is not about being mean or uncaring, but about taking care of yourself and your own well-being. When setting boundaries, it's important to be assertive, but also to be respectful and kind. This may involve explaining your reasons for setting a boundary and expressing your feelings in a calm and non-confrontational manner.

Another important aspect of setting healthy boundaries with difficult individuals is learning to communicate effectively. This may involve learning to express your needs and wants clearly and assertively, as well as learning to listen actively and empathically. For example, if a difficult individual is constantly interrupting you or talking over you, you may need to assert your right to be heard by speaking up and asking them to respect your turn to speak.

Another key element of setting healthy boundaries is learning to detach emotionally from difficult individuals. This means learning to observe and acknowledge difficult behaviors without becoming emotionally invested in them. This can be challenging, but it is an important step in protecting your own emotional well-being.

It's also important to remember that setting healthy boundaries is an ongoing process and it will require effort, patience, and a willingness to learn and grow. You may need to adjust your boundaries as you learn more about yourself and the difficult individuals in your life, and you may need to seek professional help if you are struggling to set and maintain healthy boundaries.

In conclusion, setting healthy boundaries with difficult individuals is an important aspect of self-care and maintaining healthy relationships. It requires understanding the difference between healthy and unhealthy boundaries, setting limits, clear and assertive communication, and detaching emotionally. Remember that setting boundaries is not about being mean or uncaring, but about taking care of yourself and your own well-being. It's also an ongoing process that requires effort, patience, and willingness to learn and grow. If you are struggling to set and maintain healthy boundaries, seek professional help.

It is also important to remember that setting boundaries is not always easy and it may not always be well-received by the difficult individuals in your life. They may push back, argue, or try to convince you to change your mind. It's important to be prepared for this and to stand firm in your boundaries. Remember that you have the right to set boundaries and to take care of yourself, and that the other person's behavior is not your responsibility.

It can also be helpful to practice self-care and self-compassion when setting boundaries with difficult individuals. Self-care can help you to stay grounded and focused, and it can also help you to bounce back from difficult interactions. Practice self-compassion by being kind and understanding towards yourself, and remind yourself that it is normal to struggle and make mistakes when setting boundaries.

It's also important to remember that setting boundaries is not always about ending a relationship. In some cases, it may be possible to maintain a relationship with a difficult individual while still setting healthy boundaries. For example, you may need to set boundaries with a family member or a colleague, but you may still be able to have a healthy relationship with them.

In summary, setting healthy boundaries with difficult individuals is an important aspect of self-care and maintaining healthy relationships. It requires understanding the difference between healthy and unhealthy boundaries, setting limits, clear and assertive communication, and detaching emotionally. Remember that setting boundaries is not always easy, and it may not always be well-received, but it is an ongoing process that requires effort, patience, and willingness to learn and grow. Practice self-care and self-compassion, and remember that setting boundaries is not always about ending a relationship. If you are struggling, seek professional help.

# 05: Communicating Effectively with Toxic People

Effective communication is vital in any relationship, whether it be with a colleague, a friend, or a family member. However, when dealing with toxic people, the stakes are raised and effective communication becomes even more important.

Toxic people are those who consistently engage in negative, harmful behavior, whether it be verbal or physical abuse, manipulation, or gaslighting. They can make you feel drained, frustrated, and even worthless. However, it is important to remember that while you cannot change their behavior, you can change how you respond to it.

One of the most important things to remember when communicating with toxic people is to set boundaries. This means clearly stating what you will and will not tolerate in terms of behavior, and then sticking to those boundaries. For example, if someone consistently speaks to you in a disrespectful or demeaning tone, you can let them know that you will not tolerate that kind of language and that you expect them to speak to you with respect.

## 05: COMMUNICATING EFFECTIVELY WITH TOXIC PEOPLE

Another key aspect of communicating effectively with toxic people is to remain calm and composed. It can be easy to get caught up in the emotions and drama of the situation, but doing so will only serve to fuel the toxic behavior. Instead, try to remain level-headed and stay focused on the matter at hand.

When communicating with toxic people, it is also important to be assertive, rather than aggressive or passive. Being assertive means standing up for yourself and your needs, while also being respectful of the other person. This can be difficult, especially when dealing with someone who is constantly trying to push your buttons, but it is crucial in order to maintain control of the situation.

Another effective strategy when communicating with toxic people is to use "I" statements, rather than "you" statements. For example, instead of saying "You always make me feel so small," try saying "I feel small when you speak to me that way." This puts the focus on your own feelings and experiences, rather than making accusations against the other person, which can be more likely to lead to defensiveness and conflict.

# 05: COMMUNICATING EFFECTIVELY WITH TOXIC PEOPLE

It is also important to be aware of your own triggers and emotional responses when dealing with toxic people. This means being aware of the things that tend to set you off, and learning to recognize the signs that you are becoming emotionally triggered. Once you are aware of your triggers, you can take steps to manage your emotional responses and prevent yourself from becoming further enmeshed in the toxic behavior.

In some cases, it may be necessary to cut ties with toxic people in order to protect your own mental and emotional well-being. This can be a difficult decision, but it is important to remember that you deserve to be treated with respect and kindness. If someone is consistently treating you poorly, it may be time to consider ending the relationship.

Overall, communicating effectively with toxic people requires a combination of setting boundaries, remaining calm and composed, being assertive, using "I" statements, being aware of your own triggers and emotional responses, and knowing when it is time to cut ties. While it can be challenging to deal with toxic people, by staying true to yourself and standing up for yourself, you can protect your own mental and emotional well-being and maintain your sense of self-worth.

In addition to the strategies mentioned above, there are a few other techniques that can be helpful when communicating with toxic people.

One is to use reflective listening. This means actively listening to what the other person is saying and then reflecting back to them your understanding of their words. This can help to defuse tension and show the other person that you are truly listening and trying to understand their perspective.

Another technique is to use "gray rock" method, which means being as neutral and unresponsive as possible when dealing with toxic people. This can be especially effective when dealing with someone who thrives on drama and conflict. By not giving them the emotional reaction they are looking for, you can take away their power and reduce the likelihood of them engaging in toxic behavior.

It is also important to be aware of your own body language and nonverbal cues when communicating with toxic people.

# 05: COMMUNICATING EFFECTIVELY WITH TOXIC PEOPLE

Our nonverbal cues, such as facial expressions and body posture, can communicate just as much as our words do. By being aware of your own nonverbal cues, you can make sure that they are not sending mixed signals or inadvertently encouraging toxic behavior.

It is also important to remember that toxic people are often dealing with their own issues and may not even be aware of the harm they are causing. It is not your responsibility to fix them, but it is important to communicate your own feelings and needs in a clear and assertive manner.

In any case, it is essential to protect yourself and your emotional well-being when dealing with toxic people. This may mean limiting your interactions with them, seeking support from friends and family, or seeking professional help if needed. Remember that you deserve to be treated with respect and kindness, and do not let anyone make you feel otherwise.

In conclusion, communicating effectively with toxic people requires a combination of setting boundaries, remaining calm and composed, being assertive, using "I" statements, being aware of your own triggers and emotional responses, and knowing when it is time to cut ties. It also requires being aware of your own body language and nonverbal cues, using reflective listening and "gray rock" method. It may be challenging, but by staying true to yourself and standing up for yourself, you can protect your own mental and emotional well-being and maintain your sense of self-worth.

# 06: Navigating Difficult Conversations with Toxic Individuals

Navigating difficult conversations with toxic individuals can be challenging and draining, but it is an important skill to have in order to maintain healthy relationships and protect your own well-being. In this chapter, we will discuss strategies for preparing for and handling difficult conversations with toxic individuals, as well as ways to take care of yourself after the conversation.

First and foremost, it is important to prepare for a difficult conversation with a toxic individual. This means setting clear boundaries, identifying your goals for the conversation, and practicing what you want to say. It is also helpful to anticipate potential objections or counterarguments that the other person may bring up.

When it comes to setting boundaries, it is important to be firm and clear. This means communicating your needs and expectations in a direct and non-confrontational way. For example, you could say something like "I need to have a conversation with you about your behavior, but I want to make sure we can have a productive and respectful conversation."

As for identifying your goals for the conversation, it is important to think about what you want to accomplish and what outcome you would like to see. For example, your goal may be to express your feelings, address specific behaviors, or come to a resolution. Having a clear goal in mind will help you stay focused and on track during the conversation.

Practicing what you want to say before the conversation can also be helpful. This can include writing out your thoughts or role-playing with a friend or therapist. Practicing will not only help you feel more confident and prepared, but it will also help you stay calm and focused during the actual conversation.

During the conversation, it is important to remain calm and composed. This can be difficult when dealing with a toxic individual, but it is important to remember that reacting emotionally will only escalate the situation. Instead, try to stay focused on the facts and the specific behaviors that you want to address. It's also helpful to use "I" statements, such as "I feel hurt when you speak to me in that way," instead of "you" statements, like "you always talk to me that way." This can help the other person understand how their behavior affects you, instead of putting them on the defensive.

Another important strategy for handling difficult conversations with toxic individuals is to keep the conversation focused on the present. Avoid bringing up past issues or accusations, as this will only serve to escalate the situation. Instead, stick to the specific behaviors or issues that you want to address in the present.

It's also important to be prepared for the other person to become defensive or hostile. They may try to deflect blame or responsibility, or even turn the conversation around to make it about you. In these situations, it is important to remain calm and stay focused on the specific behaviors that you want to address. It's also helpful to remind the other person that you are having this conversation because you care about them and want to see things improve.

After the conversation, it is important to take care of yourself. This may include debriefing with a trusted friend or therapist, practicing self-care activities such as exercise or meditation, or simply taking some time to relax and unwind. It's also important to reflect on the conversation and evaluate whether or not your goals were met, and if not, what you can do differently next time.

In summary, navigating difficult conversations with toxic individuals can be challenging, but with preparation, clear boundaries, and a focus on the present, it is possible to handle these conversations in a healthy and productive way. Remember to take care of yourself after the conversation and reflect on what you can do differently next time.

It's also important to remember that not every conversation or relationship with a toxic individual can be resolved or fixed. Sometimes, despite your best efforts, the other person may not be willing or able to change their behavior. In these cases, it may be necessary to distance yourself from the individual and prioritize your own well-being.

This can be a difficult and painful decision, but it is important to remember that you deserve to be treated with respect and kindness. If you find that your efforts to communicate and resolve issues with a toxic individual are not successful, it may be necessary to limit or end the relationship. This could mean setting firm boundaries, such as limiting contact or ending the relationship altogether.

## 06: NAVIGATING DIFFICULT CONVERSATIONS WITH TOXIC INDIVIDUALS

In some cases, it may be necessary to seek professional help, such as counseling or therapy. A therapist can help you work through your feelings and develop strategies for coping with a toxic individual. They can also provide support and guidance as you navigate the process of distancing yourself from the individual.

In addition, it's important to surround yourself with positive, supportive people. Spend time with friends and family who lift you up and make you feel good about yourself. Having a strong support system can help you cope with the stress and negativity that can come from interacting with a toxic individual.

In conclusion, navigating difficult conversations with toxic individuals can be challenging, but with preparation, clear boundaries, and a focus on the present, it is possible to handle these conversations in a healthy and productive way. It's important to remember to take care of yourself after the conversation, reflect on what you can do differently next time, and to be prepared to distance yourself if necessary, with the help of professional support if needed. Remember that you deserve to be treated with respect and kindness and it's important to prioritize your own well-being in any situation.

# 07: Managing Emotions in the Presence of Toxic People

Managing emotions in the presence of toxic people can be a challenging task, but it is important to remember that you are not alone and that there are strategies you can use to cope.

First, it is important to recognize when someone is toxic. A toxic person is someone who consistently engages in negative behavior, such as manipulation, gaslighting, and verbal abuse. They may also be prone to blame-shifting and spreading rumors. Additionally, toxic people often have a negative impact on those around them, including causing stress and anxiety, and diminishing self-esteem.

One strategy for coping with toxic people is to set boundaries. This means communicating to the person that their behavior is not acceptable and that you will not tolerate it. It also means setting limits on the amount of time you spend with them, and avoiding situations where you know they will be present.

Another strategy is to practice self-care. This includes taking care of your physical and emotional well-being, such as

getting enough sleep, eating well, and engaging in activities
that make you feel good. It also means being mindful of
your thoughts and emotions, and working to shift negative
thoughts to more positive ones.

Another key strategy is to build a support system. This includes surrounding yourself with people who are positive
and supportive, and seeking out professional help if needed.
Friends, family members, or a therapist can provide a
sounding board and offer guidance and advice.

In addition, it is important to focus on the things you can
control and let go of the things you can't. This means not
getting caught up in the toxic person's drama or trying to
change them, but instead focusing on your own actions and
emotions.

It is also important to remember that healing takes time. It
can be difficult to let go of the impact that a toxic person has
had on your life, but with time, patience, and the right
strategies, you can begin to move forward.

Overall, managing emotions in the presence of toxic people
is a process that requires self-awareness, boundaries, self-

care, support, and patience. Remember that you are not alone and that you deserve to be treated with respect and kindness. By focusing on your own well-being, you can begin to move past the negative impact that toxic people have had on your life, and towards a more positive and healthy future.

Another important aspect of managing emotions in the presence of toxic people is learning how to communicate effectively. This means expressing yourself clearly and assertively, without being aggressive or passive. When dealing with a toxic person, it's important to speak up for yourself and let them know how their behavior is affecting you. This can be difficult, as toxic people often use manipulation and gaslighting to control the conversation and make you doubt yourself. However, it's important to stay firm and not let them control the conversation.

It's also important to remember that not all toxic people are created equal. Some people may be toxic in certain situations, but not in others. For example, a boss who is demanding and strict may be considered toxic in a work setting, but not necessarily in other areas of their life. It's im-

portant to understand the context of the person's behavior
and address it accordingly.

Another strategy for managing emotions in the presence of
toxic people is to practice mindfulness. Mindfulness is the
ability to be present in the moment and aware of your
thoughts and emotions. This can help you stay grounded
and not get caught up in the toxic person's drama. Mindfulness techniques, such as meditation or yoga, can also help
you reduce stress and increase emotional regulation.

It's also important to remember that toxic people are not always in your life permanently. Sometimes, toxic people
come and go. It's important to not let them define your life
and take away your happiness. Remember that you deserve
to be treated with respect and kindness, and that you have
the power to choose the people you surround yourself with.

In conclusion, managing emotions in the presence of toxic
people can be a challenging task, but it's important to remember that you are not alone and that there are strategies
you can use to cope. Setting boundaries, practicing self-
care, building a support system, focusing on the things you
can control, and learning how to communicate effectively

are all important strategies for dealing with toxic people. Remember that healing takes time, but with patience and the right strategies, you can begin to move forward and create a more positive and healthy future for yourself.

# 08: Strategies for Dealing with a Toxic Boss or Colleague

Dealing with a toxic boss or colleague can be one of the most difficult and stressful situations that you will face in the workplace. A toxic individual can create a negative and harmful work environment that can have a detrimental effect on your mental and physical well-being. However, there are strategies that you can use to deal with a toxic person and protect yourself from the negative effects of their behavior.

The first step in dealing with a toxic boss or colleague is to identify the behavior that is causing the problem. This may include verbal abuse, bullying, manipulation, or other forms of mistreatment. Once you have identified the behavior, it is important to document it. Keep a detailed record of any incidents, including the date, time, and what was said or done. This will be helpful if you need to escalate the situation to higher management or take legal action.

The next step is to set boundaries with the toxic person. It is important to communicate your expectations clearly and assertively. Let them know that their behavior is unacceptable and that you will not tolerate it. It is important to be firm and assertive when setting boundaries, but also to remain professional and respectful.

Another effective strategy for dealing with a toxic boss or colleague is to build a support network. This can include talking to colleagues, friends, family, or a therapist about your experiences. Having people to talk to who understand what you are going through can help you to cope with the stress and negative effects of the toxic person's behavior.

Another good strategy is to avoid interacting with the toxic person as much as possible. This can be difficult if the person is your boss, but try to limit your interactions to only what is necessary for your job. Avoid engaging in any unnecessary conversations or interactions, and try to avoid being alone with the person.

In case the toxic person is your boss, and the situation is out of control, it might be wise to seek for a transfer or new job. This is a big step, and requires a well-thought decision process and a clear plan. But if the toxic person is making your life unbearable, it might be the best solution for you.

It's also important to remember that it's not your responsibility to change the toxic person's behavior. It's their responsibility to change their behavior, and it's important to remember that you cannot control their actions. The most important thing is to take care of yourself and protect yourself from the negative effects of their behavior.

In conclusion, dealing with a toxic boss or colleague can be a challenging and stressful situation, but there are strategies that you can use to protect yourself and manage the situation. It's important to identify the behavior, set boundaries, build a support network, avoid interacting with the toxic person as much as possible, and consider a job change if the situation is out of control. Remember, it's not your responsibility to change the toxic person's behavior, the most important thing is to take care of yourself.

Another important strategy is to maintain a positive attitude and focus on your work. It can be easy to let the toxic person's behavior consume your thoughts and emotions, but it's important to remember that you are there to do a job and to be productive. Try to focus on your tasks and goals, and don't let the toxic person's behavior distract you from what's important.

## 08: STRATEGIES FOR DEALING WITH A TOXIC BOSS OR COLLEAGUE

It's also important to seek help if you need it. If the toxic person's behavior is affecting your mental or physical health, it's important to seek professional help. This can include talking to a therapist, counselor, or employee assistance program (EAP) if your company offers one. They can provide support and guidance on how to deal with the situation and manage any negative effects it may be having on you.

Another key strategy is to communicate effectively with the toxic person. While it's important to set boundaries and avoid unnecessary interactions, there may be times when you need to communicate with the toxic person in order to resolve a work-related issue or to provide feedback. In these situations, it's important to communicate clearly and effectively, focusing on the facts and avoiding personal attacks.

Additionally, try to be proactive and come up with solutions to the problem. If the toxic person is causing issues with communication or collaboration, for example, try to come up with solutions that can improve the situation. This can include suggesting new processes or tools for communication and collaboration, or finding ways to improve team dynamics.

Finally, it's important to remember that you are not alone in dealing with a toxic boss or colleague. Many people have had to deal with similar situations, and there are resources and support available to help you. Remember to take care of yourself, set boundaries, and seek help if you need it. With the right strategies and support, you can successfully navigate this difficult situation and come out stronger on the other side.

# 09: The Role of Self-Care in Protecting Your Emotional and Mental Well-being

Self-care is a vital component of maintaining emotional and mental well-being. It refers to the actions and practices that individuals undertake to protect and promote their own health and well-being. This can include physical self-care, such as exercise and healthy eating, as well as emotional and mental self-care, such as mindfulness and self-reflection.

Physical self-care is important because it helps to maintain the body's overall health and well-being. Eating a balanced diet, getting regular exercise, and getting enough sleep are all crucial for maintaining physical health. Additionally, engaging in activities that promote relaxation, such as yoga or meditation, can also help to reduce stress and improve overall well-being.

Emotional and mental self-care are just as important as physical self-care, if not more so. Emotional self-care refers to the actions and practices that individuals undertake to protect and promote their emotional well-being. This can include things like journaling, talking to a therapist or counselor, and engaging in activities that bring joy and pleasure.

Mental self-care refers to the actions and practices that individuals undertake to protect and promote their mental well-being. This can include things like mindfulness, self-reflection, and cognitive-behavioral therapy. Mindfulness, for example, is a practice that involves paying attention to the present moment, without judgment. This can help individuals to become more aware of their thoughts and emotions, and to respond to them in a more healthy and constructive way.

Self-reflection is another important aspect of mental self-care. It involves taking the time to reflect on one's thoughts, emotions, and behaviors, and to consider how they may be impacting one's overall well-being. This can be done through journaling, talking to a therapist or counselor, or engaging in other reflective activities.

Cognitive-behavioral therapy (CBT) is a form of talk therapy that helps individuals to identify and change negative patterns of thinking and behavior. It can be particularly helpful for individuals who are struggling with anxiety, depression, or other mental health conditions.

In conclusion, self-care is essential for protecting and promoting emotional and mental well-being. It includes physical, emotional and mental practices that are aimed at maintaining and improving overall health and well-being. Engaging in self-care activities can help to reduce stress, improve
mood, and promote overall well-being. It's important to
make self-care a regular part of your daily routine, and to
prioritize it as much as possible. Remember to take care of
yourself, both physically and mentally, to ensure your well-
being.

Another important aspect of self-care is setting boundaries.
This means learning to say no to things that do not serve
your well-being and setting limits on the time and energy
you spend on others. It also includes recognizing and addressing toxic relationships and situations. Setting boundaries can be difficult, but it is important in order to protect
your emotional and mental well-being.

Another aspect of self-care is self-compassion. This means
being kind and understanding towards oneself, rather than
being self-critical. Self-compassion involves acknowledging

and accepting one's own limitations and mistakes, and treating oneself with the same kindness and understanding that one would offer to a friend. Research has shown that self-compassion is positively associated with emotional well-being and psychological health.

It's also important to take care of yourself in times of stress and crisis. This means knowing your limits and recognizing when you need to take a step back and take care of yourself. It may also mean seeking professional help or support if needed. It's important to remember that it's okay to not be okay and it's important to take the time and space to process and heal.

In summary, self-care is crucial for protecting and promoting emotional and mental well-being. It includes a variety of practices, such as physical self-care, emotional and mental self-care, setting boundaries, self-compassion and taking care of yourself in times of stress and crisis. It's important to make self-care a regular part of your daily routine, and to prioritize it as much as possible. Remember to take care of yourself, both physically and mentally, to ensure your well-being.

# 10: The Importance of Support Systems in Dealing with Toxic People

Support systems play a crucial role in helping individuals deal with toxic people. These systems can take many forms, including friends, family, therapy, support groups, and even online communities. They provide a safe space for individuals to share their experiences, receive validation and guidance, and build resilience against toxic behavior.

First and foremost, support systems can provide a sounding board for individuals to process and make sense of their experiences with toxic people. This can be particularly important for individuals who have been in toxic relationships, as they may have difficulty understanding and articulating their feelings. By sharing their experiences with a supportive listener, individuals can gain insight into their own reactions and begin to understand the dynamics of the toxic relationship.

Support systems can also provide validation for individuals' feelings and experiences. This validation can be especially important for individuals who have been gaslighted, or manipulated into doubting their own perception of reality, by a toxic person. By receiving validation from a trusted friend or therapist, individuals can begin to rebuild their sense of self and trust in their own judgment.

In addition to validation and understanding, support systems can also provide guidance and practical advice on how to navigate toxic relationships. This can include advice on setting boundaries, communicating effectively, and even strategies for ending a relationship. Support systems can also help individuals develop the resilience they need to cope with the negative effects of toxic behavior.

One important aspect of support systems is the ability to provide a sense of belonging and connection. This is particularly important for individuals who have been isolated by a toxic person. Joining a support group or online community of individuals who have also experienced toxic behavior can help individuals feel less alone and more understood. It can also provide a sense of empowerment, as individuals see that they are not alone in their experiences and can learn from the coping strategies of others.

Therapy is also an important form of support system in

dealing with toxic people. A therapist can provide a safe space for individuals to process and make sense of their experiences. They can also help individuals identify patterns in their relationships and provide guidance on how to navigate them in a healthier way. They can also help individuals develop the skills they need to build healthier relationships in the future.

Overall, support systems play a crucial role in helping individuals deal with toxic people. They provide a safe space for individuals to process and make sense of their experiences, receive validation and guidance, and build resilience against toxic behavior. Whether it is a friend, family member, therapist, support group, or online community, support systems can make all the difference in helping individuals regain their sense of self and navigate toxic relationships.

It is important to note that, while support systems can be incredibly helpful, they are not a substitute for taking action to remove oneself from a toxic situation. Support systems can provide the necessary emotional and psychological support to do so, but ultimately it is up to the individual to make the decision to leave a toxic relationship. It is also cru-

## 10: THE IMPORTANCE OF SUPPORT SYSTEMS IN DEAL-ING WITH TOXIC PEOPLE

cial to remember that healing from toxic relationships is a process that takes time, and it is important to be patient with oneself and to practice self-care during this time.

In conclusion, support systems play a crucial role in dealing with toxic people. They provide a sense of belonging, validation, guidance, and resilience, which are all essential for individuals to navigate toxic situations and regain their sense of self. It is important to remember that healing from toxic relationships is a process that takes time, and it is important to be patient with oneself and to practice self-care during this time. If you or someone you know is in a toxic relationship, seek out support systems and take the necessary steps to remove yourself from the toxic situation support from friends, family, therapy, support groups or online communities. Remember that it is not weak to ask for help, and that healing and regaining your sense of self is a journey that you don't have to go through alone.

It is also important to recognize the signs of toxic behavior and to be aware of the red flags in a relationship. This includes verbal, emotional, physical and sexual abuse, manipulation, gaslighting, and controlling behavior. It's important to trust your instincts and to take action if you feel unsafe in a relationship.

Another important aspect of support systems is to surround yourself with positive and healthy relationships. Surrounding yourself with individuals who have healthy boundaries, who respect you and your feelings and who support your growth and well-being can be incredibly beneficial. They can serve as positive role models, and can provide a sense of hope and encouragement.

One important aspect to remember is that healing takes time, and it's important not to rush the process. It's important to give yourself the time and space to process your feelings, and to work through the trauma. You may need to take a break from relationships altogether, and focus on yourself, your well-being, and your healing.

In summary, support systems play an essential role in dealing with toxic people. They provide validation, understanding, guidance, and resilience, which are all essential for individuals to navigate toxic situations and regain their sense of self. It is important to recognize the signs of toxic behavior, to be aware of red flags in relationships, and to trust your instincts. Surround yourself with positive and healthy relationships, and give yourself the time and space to heal. Remember that healing is a journey and it's important to be patient with yourself and to practice self-care.

# 11: How to Address and Resolve Conflict with Difficult Individuals

Conflict is an inevitable part of any relationship, whether it is between coworkers, family members, or friends. When dealing with difficult individuals, the key is to approach the situation with a level head and a clear plan of action.

The first step in resolving conflict with difficult individuals is to identify the root cause of the problem. This can be done by observing the individual's behavior and asking open-ended questions to gain a better understanding of their perspective. Once the root cause is identified, it is important to address the problem directly and in a non-confrontational manner. This can be achieved by using "I" statements, such as "I feel frustrated when you do X" rather than "You always do X."

Another important aspect of resolving conflict with difficult individuals is effective communication. This includes active listening, which involves paying attention to the individual's words and body language, and responding in a way that shows understanding and empathy. It is also important to avoid making assumptions and to stay focused on the issue at hand, rather than getting sidetracked by irrelevant topics.

# 11: HOW TO ADDRESS AND RESOLVE CONFLICT WITH DIFFICULT INDIVIDUALS

It is also important to set boundaries in dealing with difficult individuals. This means setting clear limits on what behavior is acceptable and what is not. This can be done by using "I" statements, such as "I will not tolerate X" or "I need Y." Setting boundaries also means being able to say "no" when necessary, and standing firm in your convictions.

Another key aspect of resolving conflict with difficult individuals is compromise. This means being willing to make concessions in order to find a mutually acceptable solution. It is important to remember that compromise does not mean giving in or giving up your own needs, but rather finding a middle ground that takes into account the needs of all parties involved.

Finally, it is important to practice self-care when dealing with difficult individuals. This means taking time for yourself to relax and recharge, and seeking support from friends, family, or a therapist when needed. It is also important to remember that you cannot change other people, but you can change your own behavior and reactions.

In conclusion, resolving conflict with difficult individuals requires a combination of effective communication, setting boundaries, compromise, and self-care. By approaching the situation with a level head and a clear plan of action, you can find a resolution that benefits everyone involved.

Another important strategy for addressing and resolving conflict with difficult individuals is to use conflict resolution techniques, such as negotiation, mediation, or arbitration. These techniques can be used to find a mutually acceptable solution to the problem and can be especially effective when the conflict is related to a specific issue, rather than a personality clash.

Negotiation involves both parties discussing their needs and wants in order to come to an agreement. This can be done through direct communication or with the help of a neutral third party. Mediation involves a neutral third party, who helps to facilitate communication between the parties and facilitates the resolution process. Arbitration is similar to mediation, but the neutral third party makes a decision for the parties, which is binding.

When dealing with difficult individuals, it is important to remain calm and professional. It is easy to become emotional or defensive when dealing with someone who is challenging, but this will only escalate the situation. Instead, try to maintain a neutral tone and avoid personal attacks.

It is also important to consider the power dynamics at play in the situation. Difficult individuals may be in a position of authority, or they may be using their power to bully or manipulate others. In these cases, it may be necessary to seek help from a supervisor or HR representative.

Finally, it is important to remember that resolving conflict with difficult individuals is a process that may require time and patience. It is not always possible to resolve the conflict in one conversation or meeting, and it may be necessary to revisit the issue at a later time.

In conclusion, addressing and resolving conflict with difficult individuals requires a combination of effective communication, setting boundaries, compromise, self-care, and conflict resolution techniques. It is important to remain calm, professional and neutral, and to consider the power dynamics at play. Remember that resolving conflict is a process that may take time and patience. With the right approach, it is possible to find a mutually acceptable solution that benefits everyone involved.

# 12: Understanding and Managing Gaslighting and Manipulation

Gaslighting and manipulation are two of the most harmful and insidious forms of emotional abuse. They are used by individuals who seek to control and dominate others, often in the context of intimate relationships or in the workplace. Understanding these behaviors and how to protect yourself from them is crucial for maintaining your mental and emotional well-being.

Gaslighting is a form of manipulation in which the abuser manipulates their victim into doubting their own reality and memory. This is done by denying or distorting events that have occurred, and by making the victim question their own perception of reality. For example, an abuser might deny that a certain conversation took place, or claim that the victim is imagining things. Over time, the victim may begin to doubt their own memory and perception of events, and may even begin to question their own sanity.

Manipulation is a form of emotional abuse that involves using deceit, guilt, or other tactics to control and dominate others. Manipulation can take many forms, including verbal manipulation, emotional manipulation, and financial manipulation. For example, an abuser might use guilt to make their victim feel responsible for their own abuse, or use deceit to make their victim trust them.

Both gaslighting and manipulation are forms of emotional abuse that can have serious consequences for the victim. They can lead to feelings of confusion, self-doubt, and even depression and anxiety. They can also lead to physical and emotional distance between the victim and their loved ones, which can further isolate the victim and make it more difficult for them to get help.

It is important to understand that gaslighting and manipulation are not the victim's fault. These behaviors are used by individuals who seek to control and dominate others, and they are not something that the victim can change. The only way to protect yourself from gaslighting and manipulation is to be aware of these behaviors and to take steps to protect yourself.

There are a few steps that you can take to protect yourself from gaslighting and manipulation. First, it is important to be aware of these behaviors and to recognize them when they occur. This can be difficult, as gaslighting and manipulation can be subtle and difficult to detect. However, by paying close attention to your interactions with others, you can begin to identify these behaviors and take action to protect yourself.

Second, it is important to set boundaries and to assert yourself. This means saying "no" when you are uncomfortable or when someone is trying to control or manipulate you. It also means standing up for yourself when someone is denying or distorting your reality. Setting boundaries is important for maintaining your mental and emotional well-being, and for preventing further abuse.

Third, it is important to seek support. This can be from friends, family, or a therapist. Talking to someone about what you are experiencing can help you to process your feelings and to develop a plan to protect yourself. It can also be helpful to seek out resources, such as books or online articles, that can provide you with more information about gaslighting and manipulation.

Finally, it is important to remember that healing is possible. While gaslighting and manipulation can be incredibly damaging, it is possible to recover and to move on. With the right support and resources, you can learn to trust yourself again and to regain your sense of self-worth.

In conclusion, gaslighting and manipulation are two of the most harmful and insidious forms of emotional abuse. They are used by individuals who seek to control and dominate others, and can have serious consequences for the victim. However, by being aware of these behaviors, setting boundaries, seeking support, and remembering that healing is possible, individuals can protect themselves from these harmful behaviors and regain control of their lives.

It's important to note that gaslighting and manipulation can happen in any type of relationship, not just romantic ones. For example, a boss or coworker may use gaslighting tactics to make an employee question their own performance or ability to do their job. It's also important to be aware that both men and women can be perpetrators or victims of gaslighting and manipulation.

Gaslighting and manipulation can also happen in a group setting, such as in a family or within a community. In these situations, the abuser may use their position of power or influence to control and manipulate the group. This can make it even harder for the victims to speak up and seek help, as they may feel like they are alone in their experience or that they will not be believed.

It's also important to understand that gaslighting and manipulation are not always intentional. Some individuals may not even be aware that they are engaging in these behaviors. However, this does not negate the harm they can cause, and it's still important for the victim to take steps to protect themselves.

If you suspect that you or someone you know is experiencing gaslighting or manipulation, it's important to reach out for help. This may include talking to a therapist or counselor, a hotlines, or a support group. It can also be helpful to research and educate yourself about the topic, as understanding the dynamics of gaslighting and manipulation can help to empower you.

It's also important to remember that leaving a gaslighting or manipulative relationship can be difficult and may be dangerous. It's important to have a safety plan in place and to seek support from professionals or trusted individuals.

## 12: UNDERSTANDING AND MANAGING GASLIGHTING AND MANIPULATION

In addition to the above, it's important to be mindful of one's own behavior and to not gaslight or manipulate others. By being aware of the dynamics of these behaviors and actively working to avoid them, we can all play a role in creating a more healthy and respectful society.

In summary, gaslighting and manipulation are forms of emotional abuse that can have serious consequences for the victim. Understanding these behaviors and taking steps to protect yourself, seeking support, and leaving a dangerous relationship if necessary is crucial for maintaining your mental and emotional well-being. Remember that healing is possible, and with the right support and resources, you can regain control of your life.

# 13: The Role of Professional Help in Dealing with Toxic People

Toxic people can be found everywhere in our lives, from the workplace to our personal relationships. They can cause significant stress and can even lead to mental health issues such as depression and anxiety. It is important to understand that toxic people are not always easy to spot and that their behavior can be subtle. It is also important to understand that toxic people can be helped, and that professional help can play a crucial role in dealing with them.

One of the main roles of professional help in dealing with toxic people is to provide support for the victim of the toxic behavior. This can include therapy or counseling sessions to help the victim process the trauma they have experienced and to develop strategies for coping with the toxic person. This might involve working on building self-esteem, learning to set boundaries, and developing a support network.

Another important role of professional help is to educate the toxic person on their behavior and its effects. This might involve therapy, counseling, or coaching sessions to help the toxic person understand the impact of their behavior on others and to develop strategies for changing their behavior.

## 13: THE ROLE OF PROFESSIONAL HELP IN DEALING WITH TOXIC PEOPLE

This can be a difficult process as toxic people often do not recognize their own toxic behavior and may be resistant to change. However, with the right approach and support, it is possible to help toxic people change their behavior and improve their relationships.

It is also important for professional help to be involved when dealing with toxic people in the workplace. This might involve working with human resources departments to develop policies and procedures for dealing with toxic behavior and to provide support for employees who are affected by it. This might also involve providing training for managers and supervisors on how to recognize and address toxic behavior in the workplace.

In addition to providing support and education, professional help can also play a role in mediation and conflict resolution. This might involve working with all parties involved to develop a plan for addressing the toxic behavior and resolving the conflict. This might also include working with the toxic person to help them understand the impact of their behavior and to develop strategies for changing it.

It is important to understand that dealing with toxic people can be a difficult and emotional process. However, with the right support and professional help, it is possible to improve the situation and to develop strategies for coping with the toxic behavior. It is also important to remember that toxic people can change and that professional help can play a crucial role in this process.

Overall, toxic people can cause significant stress and can even lead to mental health issues such as depression and anxiety. However, with the right professional help, it is possible to provide support for the victim of the toxic behavior, educate the toxic person on their behavior and its effects, involve professional help in dealing with toxic people in the workplace, and play a role in mediation and conflict resolution. Professional help is crucial in dealing with toxic people and in helping them change their behavior and improve their relationships.

Another important aspect of professional help when dealing with toxic people is the identification of underlying issues that may be contributing to the toxic behavior. This might include mental health issues such as personality disorders or unresolved past traumas that are impacting the individual's ability to form healthy relationships. Understanding these underlying issues can help in developing appropriate treatment plans and addressing the root causes of the toxic behavior.

Moreover, professional help can also be utilized to provide support for the family members and friends of the toxic person. They may also be affected by the toxic behavior and may require support to cope with the situation and to develop healthy boundaries.

It is also important for professional help to be involved in dealing with toxic relationships in personal life, such as in romantic relationships or friendships. This might involve helping the victim to safely end the relationship and to develop strategies for moving on. It might also involve working with the toxic person to address the underlying issues that may be contributing to the toxic behavior and to develop healthier relationship patterns.

In conclusion, dealing with toxic people can be challenging, but professional help can play a crucial role in addressing the problem. From providing support and education to identifying underlying issues, professional help can help toxic people change their behavior, improve their relationships, and help their family and friends to cope with the situation. It is important to remember that toxic people can change, and that with the right support, it is possible to improve the situation and develop strategies for coping with the toxic behavior. If you or someone you know is dealing with a toxic person, it is important to seek professional help to address the problem and to improve the overall well-being of all parties involved.

# 14: How to Protect Yourself from Emotional and Psychological Abuse

Emotional and psychological abuse can have devastating effects on an individual's mental and emotional well-being. It can be difficult to recognize, and even harder to escape. However, it is important to understand the signs of emotional and psychological abuse, and to take steps to protect yourself from it.

One of the first steps in protecting yourself from emotional and psychological abuse is to recognize the signs. Some common signs of emotional and psychological abuse include:

– Constant criticism or belittling

– Gaslighting (manipulating someone into doubting their own sanity)

– Isolation from friends and family

– Threats or intimidation

– Control over finances or daily activities

## 14: HOW TO PROTECT YOURSELF FROM EMOTIONAL AND PSYCHOLOGICAL ABUSE

– Physical violence or abuse

It is also important to understand that emotional and psychological abuse can take many forms, and may not always be obvious. For example, it can be subtle, such as a partner making you feel guilty for spending time with friends or family. It can also be more overt, such as a partner threatening to hurt you or someone you care about.

If you suspect that you are being emotionally or psychologically abused, it is important to seek help. This may include talking to a therapist or counselor, or seeking support from friends or family. It may also include reaching out to a domestic violence hotline or other organization that can provide assistance and support.

Another important step in protecting yourself from emotional and psychological abuse is to set boundaries. It is important to make it clear to your abuser that certain behaviors are not acceptable, and that you will not tolerate them. This may include telling your abuser that you will not tolerate verbal abuse, or that you will not put up with being isolated from friends and family. It may also include setting limits on contact with your abuser, such as refusing to take their calls or texts at certain times of the day.

It is also important to have a safety plan in place in case of emergency. This may include having a trusted friend or family member to call in case of danger, or having a plan in place to leave your abuser if necessary. You may also consider staying in a shelter or other safe place in order to protect yourself from further abuse.

It is also important to take care of yourself emotionally and physically. Emotional and psychological abuse can take a toll on your mental and emotional well-being. It is important to take steps to take care of yourself, such as practicing self-care and self-compassion. This may include things like exercise, meditation, or journaling.

It may also be helpful to find a support group or other resources where you can connect with other people who have been through similar experiences. This can be a valuable way to connect with others who understand what you are going through, and can offer support and advice.

In short, protecting yourself from emotional and psychological abuse requires recognizing the signs, seeking help, setting boundaries, having a safety plan, and taking care of yourself emotionally and physically. Remember that you are not alone, and that help is available to you. It may take time and effort, but you can heal from the effects of emotional and psychological abuse and move on to a healthier and happier life.

It's important to keep in mind that leaving an emotionally and psychologically abusive relationship may not be easy, and it may take time and effort. It's important to have a plan and to be prepared for the possibility of resistance or retaliation from your abuser. It's also important to reach out to friends, family, or professionals for support during this time. Remember, you deserve to be treated with respect and kindness, and you are not alone in this journey.

Additionally, it is important to address any underlying issues that may have contributed to the abuse. This may include working on personal or relationship issues, or addressing any mental health concerns. It may also involve addressing any financial or legal issues that may have contributed to the abuse.

It is also important to remember that healing is a process

and it takes time. Be kind and compassionate towards yourself, and give yourself the time and space you need to heal. It is important to understand that the healing process may not be linear and you may experience ups and downs along the way.

Another important thing to keep in mind is that it's not your fault that you are being emotionally and psychologically abused. The abuser is solely responsible for their behavior and you are not to blame. It is important to understand that the abuse is not your fault, and that you deserve to be treated with respect and kindness.

It is also important to be aware of the cycle of abuse. Abusive relationships often follow a pattern of tension-building, incident, and reconciliation. The abuser may apologize and promise to change, but the cycle of abuse often repeats itself. It's important to be aware of this pattern and to recognize that the abuser may not change their behavior permanently.

In conclusion, protecting yourself from emotional and psychological abuse requires recognizing the signs, seeking help, setting boundaries, having a safety plan, taking care of yourself emotionally and physically, addressing underlying issues, being patient with yourself during the healing process, understanding that the abuse is not your fault, and being aware of the cycle of abuse. Remember that you deserve to be treated with respect and kindness, and that help is available to you. It may take time and effort, but you can heal from the effects of emotional and psychological abuse and move on to a healthier and happier life.

# 15: How to Deal with Narcissistic or Sociopathic Behavior

Dealing with narcissistic or sociopathic behavior can be a difficult and trying experience. These individuals possess a unique set of personality traits that can make them both charming and manipulative, which can make it hard to detect and cope with their behavior. In this chapter, we will discuss strategies for identifying and managing narcissistic or sociopathic behavior, as well as some tips for protecting yourself and your loved ones.

First, it is important to understand the difference between narcissism and sociopathy. Narcissism is characterized by an inflated sense of self-importance, a lack of empathy, and a need for admiration and validation. Narcissists often display grandiose behavior, such as boasting about their accomplishments or exaggerating their abilities. They may also have a strong sense of entitlement, believing that they are entitled to special treatment or privileges.

Sociopathy, on the other hand, is characterized by a lack of empathy, remorse, or guilt. Sociopaths often display impulsive and reckless behavior, and may engage in criminal or antisocial behavior. They may also be manipulators, using charm and deceit to get what they want.

One of the most important things to remember when deal-ing with narcissistic or sociopathic behavior is to protect yourself. This can mean setting boundaries, such as not al-lowing them to control your emotions or decisions. It can also mean limiting your contact with them, or avoiding them altogether if possible.

Another key strategy is to learn to recognize the signs of narcissistic or sociopathic behavior. This may include things like grandiose language, a lack of empathy, or a tendency to blame others for their problems. If you suspect that someone is displaying narcissistic or sociopathic behavior, it is important to take note of their actions and behavior.

If you find yourself in a relationship with a narcissist or so-ciopath, it can be helpful to seek the help of a therapist or counselor. These professionals can help you understand the dynamics of the relationship and provide you with tools and strategies for coping. They may also be able to provide you with support and guidance as you work to extricate yourself from the relationship.

# 15: HOW TO DEAL WITH NARCISSISTIC OR SO-CIOPATHIC BEHAVIOR

It's also important to remember that you cannot change the behavior of a narcissist or sociopath. They are unlikely to change their behavior, even if you try to educate them about the consequences of their actions. Therefore, it is important to focus on protecting yourself and your loved ones, rather than trying to change them.

In addition to these strategies, it is also important to take care of yourself emotionally and physically. This can include things like getting enough sleep, eating well, and engaging in regular exercise. Taking care of yourself will help to build your resilience and give you the energy and strength you need to deal with difficult situations.

It's also important to have a support system in place. This can include friends, family, or a therapist. These people can provide you with emotional support and help you to process your feelings about the situation.

In conclusion, dealing with narcissistic or sociopathic behavior can be a challenging experience. However, by learning to recognize the signs of this behavior and taking steps to protect yourself, you can make the process easier. Remember to set boundaries, seek professional help, take care of yourself and have a support system in place. Remember that changing the person is not possible, but you can change how you react and respond to their behavior.

It is also important to understand that not everyone who displays narcissistic or sociopathic traits is necessarily a "narcissist" or "sociopath" in the clinical sense. These terms are often used colloquially to describe individuals who exhibit certain traits, but true narcissistic personality disorder or sociopathy are considered serious mental health conditions that are diagnosed by a mental health professional. It's important to keep this in mind and not label someone too quickly, instead focus on the behavior and how it affects you and those around you.

It's also important to understand that these individuals may not even be aware of their behavior, or they may have a different perspective on it. They may not see their actions as harmful or manipulative, and may not understand why others are upset. It's important to approach these situations with empathy and understanding, while still standing up for yourself and setting boundaries.

Another important thing to remember is that the narciss-

# 15: HOW TO DEAL WITH NARCISSISTIC OR SO-CIOPATHIC BEHAVIOR

istic or sociopathic behavior can be cyclical. They may be charming and attentive one moment, and then cold and dismissive the next. This can make it difficult to predict their behavior and can leave you feeling confused and hurt. It's important to be aware of this cycle and to not take their behavior personally.

It's also important to remember that a person's behavior can be influenced by many factors, including past experiences, trauma, or mental health conditions. It's important to not judge someone based on their behavior and to have compassion for the person.

In situations where the narcissistic or sociopathic behavior is severe, it may be necessary to take legal action, such as seeking a restraining order. This can be a difficult decision to make, but it's important to remember that your safety and well-being come first.

In conclusion, dealing with narcissistic or sociopathic behavior can be a challenging experience. However, by learning to recognize the signs of this behavior, setting boundaries, seeking professional help, and taking care of yourself and your support system, you can make the process easier. Remember to approach the situation with empathy and understanding and to not take the behavior personally. If necessary, take legal action to protect yourself and your loved ones. It's important to remember that you deserve to be treated with respect and kindness, and you should never tolerate behavior that is harmful or manipulative.

# 16: How to Move On and Let Go of a Toxic Relationship

Moving on from a toxic relationship can be a challenging and difficult process. However, it is important to remember that you deserve to be in a healthy and loving relationship. Letting go of a toxic relationship is the first step towards finding the happiness and fulfillment that you deserve.

The first step in moving on from a toxic relationship is to recognize that the relationship is toxic. This may seem obvious, but it can be difficult to identify toxic behaviors when you are in the midst of a relationship. Some common signs of a toxic relationship include feeling constantly criticized, belittled, or controlled; feeling like you can never do anything right; feeling like you are walking on eggshells; or feeling like you are constantly apologizing.

Once you have recognized that the relationship is toxic, it is important to set boundaries. This may mean setting limits on how much time you spend with your partner, or it may mean ending the relationship altogether. It is important to remember that you deserve to be treated with respect and kindness, and that you should not have to put up with toxic behaviors.

It is also important to practice self-care during this time. This may mean taking time for yourself to do things that you enjoy, such as reading, exercising, or spending time with friends and family. It may also mean seeking professional help, such as counseling or therapy, to process your feelings and work through the trauma of the toxic relationship.

It is also important to work on yourself and your own personal growth during this time. This may mean taking classes or workshops to improve your communication skills, learning to set boundaries, or working on building self-esteem. Remember that a toxic relationship can leave deep scars, and it is important to take the time to heal and grow as a person.

It is also important to surround yourself with supportive people during this time. This may mean reaching out to friends and family, or it may mean joining a support group for people who have been in toxic relationships. The support and encouragement of others can be invaluable as you work through the process of moving on and letting go of a toxic relationship.

Finally, it is important to remember that letting go of a toxic relationship is a process, and it may take time. It is important to be patient with yourself and to allow yourself the time and space to heal. It is also important to remember that it is possible to move on and find happiness and fulfillment in a new relationship.

In conclusion, moving on from a toxic relationship can be a challenging and difficult process, but it is important to remember that you deserve to be in a healthy and loving relationship. Recognizing the toxic behaviors and setting boundaries, practicing self-care, working on personal growth, surrounding yourself with supportive people and allowing yourself time to heal are the key steps towards finding the happiness and fulfillment that you deserve. It is important to remember that letting go of a toxic relationship is a process and it may take time, but it is possible to move on and find happiness in a new relationship.

It is also important to understand that leaving a toxic relationship does not mean that you have failed. It is not a sign of weakness to walk away from a relationship that is not healthy or fulfilling. It takes a great deal of strength and courage to recognize when a relationship is toxic and to make the decision to leave.

It is also important to remember that healing from a toxic relationship is not a linear process. You may have good days where you feel strong and empowered, and you may have bad days where you feel overwhelmed and sad. This is normal, and it is important to be kind and compassionate towards yourself during this time.

One of the most important things to remember when moving on from a toxic relationship is that it is not your fault. Toxic relationships often involve manipulation, gaslighting, and blame-shifting. It can be easy to internalize this blame and to believe that you are responsible for the problems in the relationship. It is important to remind yourself that the problems in the relationship are not your fault and that you are not responsible for the toxic behaviors of your partner.

It is also important to recognize that healing from a toxic relationship can be a lifelong process. It may take time to fully process your feelings and to learn to trust yourself and others again. It is important to be patient with yourself and to remember that healing is not a destination, but a journey.

## 16: HOW TO MOVE ON AND LET GO OF A TOXIC RELATIONSHIP

In the end, moving on from a toxic relationship can be a difficult and challenging process, but it is also an opportunity for growth and self-discovery. It is a chance to learn about yourself, your needs, and what you truly deserve in a relationship. It is a chance to start a new chapter in your life and to find the happiness and fulfillment that you deserve. Remember to be kind and compassionate towards yourself, and to surround yourself with supportive people. Remember that you deserve love and respect, and that you are not alone in your journey.

# 17: The Importance of Forgiveness and Self-Compassion in Healing

Forgiveness and self-compassion are two essential elements of healing, both physically and emotionally. They are closely related, and both play a crucial role in our ability to let go of the past and move forward in a positive and healthy way. In this chapter, we will explore the importance of forgiveness and self-compassion in healing, and how they can be used together to help us overcome the challenges that life throws our way.

Forgiveness is the act of letting go of negative feelings towards someone who has wronged us. It is a powerful tool that can help us to release the anger, resentment, and hurt that we may be holding onto. Forgiveness allows us to let go of the past and move forward in a positive and healthy way. It is not about forgetting what has happened, but rather about acknowledging that it has happened and choosing to release the negative emotions associated with it.

Self-compassion is the act of being kind and understanding towards ourselves when we make mistakes or experience difficult emotions. It is the ability to acknowledge that we are human and that we all make mistakes. Self-compassion

# 17: THE IMPORTANCE OF FORGIVENESS AND SELF-COMPASSION IN HEALING

allows us to be kind and understanding towards ourselves, rather than judging ourselves harshly for our mistakes or shortcomings. It helps us to accept ourselves for who we are and to recognize that we are not alone in our struggles.

Forgiveness and self-compassion are closely related because they both involve the ability to let go of negative emotions and to be kind and understanding towards ourselves and others. Forgiveness allows us to let go of negative emotions towards others, while self-compassion allows us to let go of negative emotions towards ourselves. Together, they can help us to overcome the challenges that life throws our way and to move forward in a positive and healthy way.

Forgiveness is especially important in the context of healing because it allows us to release the negative emotions associated with a traumatic event or experience. Traumatic events can leave us feeling angry, resentful, and hurt, and these negative emotions can be very difficult to overcome. Forgiveness allows us to let go of these negative emotions and to move forward in a positive and healthy way.

Self-compassion is also important in the context of healing because it allows us to be kind and understanding towards ourselves when we are going through difficult times. When we are experiencing difficult emotions, it is easy to judge ourselves harshly and to blame ourselves for our struggles. Self-compassion allows us to recognize that we are human and that we all make mistakes. It helps us to accept ourselves for who we are and to recognize that we are not alone in our struggles.

Forgiveness and self-compassion are both essential elements of healing, and they can be used together to help us overcome the challenges that life throws our way. Forgiveness allows us to let go of negative emotions towards others, while self-compassion allows us to let go of negative emotions towards ourselves. Together, they can help us to move forward in a positive and healthy way.

To practice forgiveness, one can start with writing a letter of forgiveness to the person who has wronged you, even if you never plan to give or send the letter. It can help you to express your feelings and to let go of the negative emotions that you may be holding onto. You can also practice forgiveness by thinking about the situation from the other person's perspective and trying to understand why they may have acted the way they did.

To practice self-compassion, one can start by being kind and understanding towards yourself when you make mistakes or experience difficult emotions. Instead of judging yourself harshly, try to recognize that you are human and that we all make mistakes. Try to talk to yourself the way you would talk to a friend going through a similar situation. Speak to yourself with kindness and understanding, and remind yourself that it is normal to struggle and make mistakes.

Another way to practice self-compassion is through mindfulness. When experiencing difficult emotions, take a moment to observe them without judgment. Acknowledge them, and try to understand where they are coming from. This allows us to separate ourselves from our emotions and to understand that they are not a reflection of our worth as a person.

It's also important to remember that forgiveness and self-compassion are ongoing practices. They are not one-time events, and it is important to continue to work on them throughout our lives. It's also important to remember that

forgiveness and self-compassion may not be easy or immediate. It may take time and effort to work through difficult
emotions and to let go of the past.

In conclusion, forgiveness and self-compassion are essential
elements of healing, both physically and emotionally. They
allow us to let go of negative emotions, to be kind and understanding towards ourselves and others, and to move forward in a positive and healthy way. By practicing forgiveness and self-compassion, we can overcome the challenges
that life throws our way and live a more fulfilling and satisfying life.

# 18: Building Resilience and Em-powerment in the Face of Toxic People

Building resilience and empowerment in the face of toxic people can be a challenging task, but it is essential for maintaining a healthy and fulfilling life. Toxic people can come in many forms, such as a controlling partner, a manipulative friend, or a toxic coworker. They can drain your energy, make you doubt yourself, and even cause you physical and emotional harm.

To build resilience and empowerment in the face of toxic people, it is important to first identify the toxic behavior and understand how it affects you. Some common signs of toxic behavior include manipulation, gaslighting, verbal abuse, and controlling behavior. Once you have identified the toxic behavior, it is essential to set boundaries and communicate them effectively. This can include saying "no" when you feel uncomfortable or setting limits on how much time you spend with the toxic person.

Another important aspect of building resilience and empowerment is to focus on self-care. This can include practices such as exercise, meditation, journaling, and therapy. Taking care of your physical and mental health can help you build the strength and resilience you need to cope with toxic people.

It is also important to surround yourself with supportive people who uplift and encourage you. These people can serve as a source of strength and inspiration when you are dealing with toxic individuals. They can also provide a sounding board for your thoughts and feelings, which can be especially helpful when dealing with a toxic person.

Another key step to building resilience and empowerment is learning to speak up for yourself. This can be difficult, especially if you have been in a long-term relationship with a toxic person, but it is essential for breaking free from their control. Speak up for yourself, stand up for what you believe in, and don't be afraid to seek help if you need it.

Finally, it's important to remember that healing from toxic relationships takes time. You may feel overwhelmed and frustrated at times, but it's important to be patient with yourself and remember that progress is not always linear. It's important to take the time you need to heal and process your experiences before moving forward.

In conclusion, building resilience and empowerment in the face of toxic people can be challenging, but it is essential for maintaining a healthy and fulfilling life. By identifying toxic behavior, setting boundaries, focusing on self-care, surrounding yourself with supportive people, speaking up for yourself, and being patient with yourself during the healing process, you can build the resilience and empowerment you need to stand up to toxic individuals and take control of your life.

It is also important to remember that toxic people can often be experts in manipulation and gaslighting, and may try to blame you for their behavior or make you feel like you are the problem. It is crucial to understand that the problem is not with you, but with their toxic behavior. It is important to believe in yourself and your own experiences, and not let a toxic person convince you otherwise.

Another way to build resilience and empowerment is to practice assertiveness. Assertiveness is the ability to stand up for yourself and your needs while also respecting the rights and needs of others. It is important to be able to express yourself clearly and directly without being aggressive or passive. This can be helpful in communicating boundaries and standing up for yourself in the face of toxic behavior.

It is also important to remember that toxic people often have a pattern of behavior and it is unlikely that they will change. It is important to not waste your time and energy trying to change them or fix them. Instead, focus on taking care of yourself and creating a fulfilling life for yourself. It may be necessary to end the relationship with a toxic person in order to move on and heal.

In addition to all these steps, it's also important to seek professional help if you need it. A therapist or counselor can help you to process your experiences, cope with the aftermath of a toxic relationship, and develop healthy coping mechanisms. They can also help you to identify patterns of behavior in toxic relationships, so that you can avoid falling into the same trap in the future.

In summary, building resilience and empowerment in the face of toxic people is a process that requires patience, self-care, and the support of others. By identifying toxic behavior, setting boundaries, focusing on self-care, surrounding

## 18: BUILDING RESILIENCE AND EMPOWERMENT IN THE FACE OF TOXIC PEOPLE

yourself with supportive people, speaking up for yourself, practicing assertiveness, seeking professional help, and being patient with yourself during the healing process, you can build the resilience and empowerment you need to stand up to toxic individuals and take control of your life. Remember that healing takes time and it's important to be kind and compassionate with yourself during the process.

# Book 2 - Verbally Abusive Relationships

Navigating the Trauma and Complexities of Verbally Abusive Relationships: Understanding the Patterns of Emotional Manipulation and Psychological Abuse, Learning to Recognize the Warning Signs, and Developing the Skills to Break Free and Heal

# 01: Introduction: Understanding the Scope and Impact of Verbally Abusive Relationships

Verbally abusive relationships are those in which one partner uses words as a weapon to control, demean, or harm the other partner. These types of relationships can have a profound and long-lasting impact on the victim, affecting their self-esteem, mental health, and overall well-being.

Verbal abuse can take many forms, including but not limited to: name-calling, belittling, threatening, blaming, and manipulation. It can happen in any kind of relationship, including romantic partnerships, friendships, and family dynamics. It can also occur in both in-person and online interactions.

One of the most insidious aspects of verbal abuse is that it can be subtle and difficult to recognize. The abuser may use "gaslighting" tactics, where they manipulate the victim into doubting their own perceptions and memories. This can make it difficult for the victim to understand that they are being abused and to seek help.

The effects of verbal abuse can be severe and long-lasting. It can lead to a range of mental health problems such as depression, anxiety, and post-traumatic stress disorder (PTSD). It can also affect physical health, as the constant stress of verbal abuse can weaken the immune system.

Victims of verbal abuse may also develop unhealthy coping mechanisms, such as substance abuse, self-harm, and eating disorders. They may also struggle with trust issues and have difficulty forming healthy relationships in the future.

It is important to remember that verbal abuse is never the fault of the victim. No one deserves to be treated this way and it is never okay for someone to use words as a weapon to control or harm another person.

If you or someone you know is experiencing verbal abuse, it is important to seek help. This can include talking to a therapist or counselor, joining a support group, or reaching out to a hotline for advice and support. It is also important to set boundaries with the abuser and to have a plan in place for leaving the relationship if necessary.

It is also crucial to recognize that verbal abuse is not limited to any specific gender, race, or socioeconomic class, it can happen to anyone. It is important to be aware of the warning signs of verbal abuse, such as a partner who belittles or controls you, and to take action if you or someone you know is experiencing it.

In conclusion, verbal abuse is a serious issue that can have a profound and long-lasting impact on the victim. It can take many forms and can be difficult to recognize. If you or someone you know is experiencing verbal abuse, it is important to seek help and to take steps to leave the relationship if necessary. Remember that you are never at fault for being verbally abused and that you deserve to be treated with respect and kindness.

It is also important to remember that verbal abuse is not limited to romantic relationships. It can also occur in friendships and family dynamics. In these cases, the abuse can be even more insidious, as the victim may feel a sense of loyalty or obligation to the abuser.

In addition, verbal abuse in the workplace is also a serious issue. It can take the form of harassment, bullying, or discrimination, and can create a hostile work environment for the victim. Verbal abuse in the workplace can also lead to decreased job performance, increased absenteeism, and even job loss.

Verbal abuse can also happen in the form of cyberbullying, which is bullying that occurs through electronic technology, such as social media, text messages, and online forums. This type of abuse can be just as harmful as in-person verbal abuse, and it can be even more difficult to escape, as the abuser may be able to track the victim's online activity.

It is crucial to understand that verbal abuse is not just a minor disagreement or a "lover's spat." It is a pattern of be-havior that is used to control, demcan, and harm the victim. It is not acceptable, and it is not something that should be tolerated.

It is important to educate ourselves and others about the signs and effects of verbal abuse. By raising awareness, we can help to break the cycle of abuse and support those who are affected by it.

If you or someone you know is experiencing verbal abuse, it is important to seek help. Reach out to a therapist or coun-selor, a support group, or a hotline for advice and support.

## 01: INTRODUCTION: UNDERSTANDING THE SCOPE AND IMPACT OF VERBALLY ABUSIVE RELATIONSHIPS

Remember that you are not alone, and that there are people who care about you and want to help.

In conclusion, verbal abuse is a serious and pervasive issue that can affect anyone, regardless of gender, race, or socioeconomic class. It is important to understand the scope and impact of verbal abuse, and to take action to help those who are affected by it. By raising awareness and supporting victims, we can work towards a future where verbal abuse is not tolerated and where everyone is treated with respect and kindness.

# 02: The Patterns of Emotional Manipulation and Psychological Abuse

Emotional manipulation and psychological abuse are patterns of behavior that are used to control and exploit another person. These patterns often occur in relationships where one person has more power or influence than the other, such as in romantic relationships, parent-child relationships, or employer-employee relationships.

One common pattern of emotional manipulation is gaslighting, which is a form of manipulation in which the manipulator seeks to make the victim doubt their own sanity or reality. This can be done by denying that certain events occurred, or by twisting the facts of a situation to make the victim question their own perception of events. Gaslighting can be incredibly damaging to a person's mental health and self-esteem, and can leave them feeling confused and isolated.

Another pattern of emotional manipulation is love bombing, which is a form of manipulation in which the manipulator showers the victim with excessive attention and affection in the early stages of a relationship. This can make the victim feel special and desired, and can create a strong emotional bond between the two people. However, the manipulator may then withdraw this attention and affection in order to control the victim and make them do what the manipulator wants.

Another pattern of emotional manipulation is playing the victim. This is when the manipulator plays the victim in order to gain sympathy or to avoid responsibility for their own actions. They may exaggerate or fabricate their own suffering in order to gain sympathy and to make the other person feel guilty for not helping them.

Another pattern of emotional manipulation is triangulation, which is a form of manipulation in which the manipulator uses a third party to control the victim. This can be done by using another person to create jealousy or to create a sense of competition between the victim and the third party.

Another pattern of emotional manipulation is the silent treatment, which is a form of manipulation in which the manipulator ignores the victim in order to punish them or to control their behavior. This can be incredibly damaging to a person's mental health and self-esteem, and can leave them feeling confused and isolated.

Another pattern of emotional manipulation is scapegoating, which is a form of manipulation in which the manipulator blames the victim for their own mistakes or for the problems in the relationship. This can make the victim feel guilty and responsible for things that are not their fault, and can be incredibly damaging to their self-esteem.

These are just a few examples of the patterns of emotional manipulation and psychological abuse. It is important to remember that these patterns of behavior can be subtle and difficult to recognize, and that they can be used in a variety of different relationships. If you suspect that you or someone you know is being emotionally manipulated or psychologically abused, it is important to seek help and support.

In conclusion, emotional manipulation and psychological abuse are patterns of behavior that are used to control and exploit another person. They can be subtle and difficult to recognize, but it is important to be aware of the signs and to seek help if you suspect that you or someone you know is being emotionally manipulated or psychologically abused. It is important to understand that these patterns of behavior are unacceptable, and that it is never too late to seek help and to reclaim control of your life.

Another pattern of emotional manipulation is the use of ultimatums, which is when the manipulator gives the victim a choice between two options, both of which are unpleasant or undesirable. This can be used to force the victim into making a decision that they would not have made otherwise, or to control their behavior.

Another pattern of emotional manipulation is the use of guilt and shame, which is when the manipulator makes the victim feel guilty or ashamed for their actions or thoughts. This can be used to control their behavior or to make them do something they do not want to do.

Another pattern of emotional manipulation is the use of fear and intimidation, which is when the manipulator uses fear or intimidation to control the victim. This can be done by threatening harm, or by making the victim believe that something bad will happen if they do not comply with the manipulator's demands.

## 02: THE PATTERNS OF EMOTIONAL MANIPULATION AND PSYCHOLOGICAL ABUSE

Another pattern of emotional manipulation is the use of isolation, which is when the manipulator isolates the victim from friends, family, or support networks. This can be done by moving away, or by limiting the victim's access to transportation or communication.

Finally, another pattern of emotional manipulation is the use of projection, which is when the manipulator projects their own negative feelings or actions onto the victim. This can be done by accusing the victim of things the manipulator is guilty of or by making the victim believe they are the one with a problem.

It's important to understand that these patterns of emotional manipulation and psychological abuse can have long-lasting effects on the victim's mental and emotional well-being. It can lead to depression, anxiety, low self-esteem, and even post-traumatic stress disorder. It's crucial for victims to understand that they are not at fault for being manipulated and that it's not their responsibility to fix the manipulator. It is important for victims to reach out for help and support, whether it be from friends and family, or from professional therapists or counselors.

## 02: THE PATTERNS OF EMOTIONAL MANIPULATION AND PSYCHOLOGICAL ABUSE

In conclusion, emotional manipulation and psychological abuse are patterns of behavior that are used to control and exploit another person. They can be subtle, and difficult to recognize but with knowledge and awareness, one can learn to identify and protect oneself from these harmful behaviors. It is important to remember that no one deserves to be emotionally manipulated or psychologically abused, and that help is available to those who need it. It's never too late to reclaim control of your life and to heal from the trauma caused by emotional manipulation and psychological abuse.

# 03: Recognizing the Warning Signs of Verbal Abuse

Recognizing the Warning Signs of Verbal Abuse

Verbal abuse is a form of emotional abuse that involves the use of words to control, manipulate, or demean an individual. It can take many forms, including name-calling, belittling, threatening, and blaming. Verbal abuse can have a devastating impact on the victim's self-esteem, mental health, and overall well-being. In some cases, it can even lead to physical abuse.

One of the most important things to understand about verbal abuse is that it is not always obvious. It can be subtle and insidious, making it difficult for the victim to recognize. This is why it is so important to be aware of the warning signs of verbal abuse.

Here are some common warning signs of verbal abuse:

– Name-calling: Verbal abusers often use name-calling as a way to demean and belittle their victims. This can include calling them names like "stupid," "lazy," or "ugly."

– Put-downs: Verbal abusers will often make negative comments about their victims in order to undermine their confidence and self-esteem. This can include put-downs about their appearance, intelligence, or abilities.

– Threatening language: Verbal abusers may use threatening language in order to control their victims. This can include threats of harm, either physical or emotional.

– Blaming: Verbal abusers will often blame their victims for their own behavior. They may accuse their victims of causing problems or being responsible for their own abuse.

– Isolation: Verbal abusers may try to isolate their victims from friends and family in order to control and manipulate them.

– Gaslighting: Verbal abuse can also involve gaslighting, a form of psychological manipulation in which the abuser makes the victim question their own sanity or perception of reality.

– Controlling language: Verbal abusers may use controlling language to manipulate their victims and make them feel like they have no control over their own lives.

# 03: RECOGNIZING THE WARNING SIGNS OF VERBAL ABUSE

– Constant criticism: Verbal abuse can also take the form of constant criticism, where the abuser is always pointing out what the victim is doing wrong and never acknowledging when they do something right.

– Yelling or Screaming: Verbal abuse can be loud, aggressive, and scary. It can include yelling or screaming at the victim as a way to intimidate them.

– Passive-aggressive behavior: Verbal abuse can also involve passive-aggressive behavior, where the abuser makes indirect or subtle threats or insults.

It is important to remember that verbal abuse is not always obvious and can be subtle. The victim may not even realize they are being abused. The above warning signs are not exhaustive, and there may be other signs of verbal abuse. It is also important to note that verbal abuse can occur in any relationship, including romantic relationships, familial relationships, and friendships.

If you suspect that you or someone you know is being verbally abused, it is important to seek help. This can include talking to a therapist, a domestic violence advocate, or a trusted friend or family member. Remember that you are not alone and that there is help available.

In conclusion, verbal abuse is a form of emotional abuse that can have a devastating impact on the victim's self-esteem, mental health, and overall well-being. It is important to be aware of the warning signs of verbal abuse, including name-calling, put-downs, threatening language, blaming, isolation, gaslighting, controlling language, constant criticism, yelling or screaming, and passive-aggressive behavior. If you suspect that you or someone you know is being verbally abused, it is important to seek help and support.

It is also important to understand that verbal abuse is not acceptable and that the victim is not at fault for the abuse. The abuser is responsible for their own behavior and needs to take responsibility for their actions. No one deserves to be verbally abused and it is not something that should be tolerated or ignored.

It is also important to remember that healing from verbal abuse can take time and may involve working through feelings of guilt, shame, and self-doubt. It is important to be patient with yourself and to surround yourself with people who support and believe in you.

In addition to seeking help and support, it is also important to set boundaries and to communicate these boundaries clearly to the abuser. This can include telling the abuser that their behavior is not acceptable and that you will not tolerate it. It may also involve setting limits on contact with the abuser or ending the relationship altogether.

It is also important to understand that verbal abuse can have long-term effects on mental and physical health. It is important to take care of yourself both physically and emotionally. This can include engaging in self-care activities, such as exercise, healthy eating, and spending time with friends and family.

In conclusion, recognizing the warning signs of verbal abuse is crucial in order to protect yourself and others from the devastating effects of this form of emotional abuse. It is important to seek help and support, set boundaries, and take care of yourself both physically and emotionally. Remember that you deserve to be treated with respect and kindness, and that help is available.

# 04: The Trauma of Verbally Abusive Relationships

Verbally abusive relationships can have a devastating impact on a person's mental and emotional well-being. The trauma of experiencing verbal abuse can be long-lasting and can affect a person's ability to trust others, form healthy relationships, and feel safe in the world.

Verbal abuse is a form of emotional abuse that involves the use of words to manipulate, control, and demean a person. It can take many forms, including yelling, criticism, name-calling, blaming, and threatening. The abuser may use verbal abuse to assert power and control over their partner, to make the partner feel small and worthless, or to silence and dismiss their partner's thoughts and feelings.

The effects of verbal abuse can be profound and far-reaching. A person who has been verbally abused may experience feelings of worthlessness, guilt, and shame. They may also develop anxiety, depression, and post-traumatic stress disorder (PTSD). The constant emotional turmoil of verbal abuse can also lead to physical health problems, such as headaches, stomach problems, and insomnia.

## 04: THE TRAUMA OF VERBALLY ABUSIVE RELATION-SHIPS

The psychological effects of verbal abuse can be particularly damaging. A person who has been verbally abused may begin to doubt their own perceptions and thoughts, and may start to believe the negative things their abuser says about them. They may also develop a fear of their abuser and may feel trapped in the relationship.

One of the most harmful effects of verbal abuse is that it can erode a person's self-esteem and self-worth. Over time, the constant criticism and belittling can make a person feel like they are not good enough and that they will never be able to please their abuser. This can lead to feelings of hopelessness and helplessness, and can make it difficult for a person to leave an abusive relationship.

It is important to understand that verbal abuse is not just about the words that are spoken. It is about the intent behind those words. The abuser uses words as a weapon to control and manipulate their partner, and to make their partner feel small and worthless. The abuser may also use verbal abuse to silence their partner and to dismiss their partner's thoughts and feelings.

It can be difficult for a person who has been verbally abused to recognize that they are in an abusive relationship. They may make excuses for their abuser's behavior, or they may blame themselves for the abuse. They may also be afraid to leave the relationship because they fear their abuser's reaction.

It is important for a person who has been verbally abused to seek help. This can include talking to a therapist or counselor, joining a support group for survivors of verbal abuse, or speaking with a trusted friend or family member.

It is also important to understand that healing from verbal abuse is a process that takes time. A person who has been verbally abused may need to work through their feelings of worthlessness and shame, and may need to learn how to trust others again. It is also important for them to learn how to set boundaries and to communicate their needs in a healthy way.

In conclusion, verbal abuse is a form of emotional abuse that can have a devastating impact on a person's mental and emotional well-being. The effects of verbal abuse can be long-lasting and can affect a person's ability to trust others, form healthy relationships, and feel safe in the world. It is important for a person who has been verbally abused to seek help and to understand that healing is a process that takes time.

It is also important to note that verbal abuse can happen in any type of relationship, not just romantic relationships. Verbal abuse can occur in friendships, family relationships, and even in professional relationships. It is not limited to any specific gender, sexual orientation, race, or socioeconomic status.

It is important for individuals to understand the signs of verbal abuse and to be able to recognize it when it happens. Signs of verbal abuse can include:

Constant criticism and belittling

Yelling and name-calling

Blaming and gaslighting

Threatening and intimidation

Dismissing or silencing a person's thoughts and feelings

It is also important for individuals to understand that verbal abuse is not just about the words that are spoken. It is about the intent behind those words. The abuser uses words as a weapon to control and manipulate their partner, and to make their partner feel small and worthless.

It is important for individuals to have a support system in place. This can include friends, family members, and professionals who can provide emotional support and guidance. They can also help an individual to stay safe, and to leave an abusive relationship if necessary.

It is also important for individuals to understand that healing from verbal abuse is a process that takes time. A person who has been verbally abused may need to work through their feelings of worthlessness and shame, and may need to learn how to trust others again. It is also important for them to learn how to set boundaries and to communicate their needs in a healthy way.

It is also important for individuals to understand that leaving an abusive relationship is not easy and it can be dangerous. It is important to have a plan in place and to reach out for help if necessary. It is also important to understand that healing from verbal abuse is a process that takes time.

It is also important for society to understand the impact of verbal abuse and to take it seriously. This includes recognizing that verbal abuse is a form of emotional abuse and that it can have a devastating impact on a person's mental and emotional well-being. It also includes holding individuals who engage in verbal abuse accountable for their actions and to provide support for survivors of verbal abuse.

In conclusion, verbal abuse is a form of emotional abuse that can have a devastating impact on a person's mental and emotional well-being. It is important for individuals to understand the signs of verbal abuse, to have a support system in place, and to understand that healing from verbal abuse is a process that takes time. It is also important for society to take verbal abuse seriously and to provide support for survivors. By raising awareness and providing support, we can work towards ending the cycle of verbal abuse and helping survivors to heal.

# 05: The Complexities of Leaving a Verbally Abusive Relationship

Leaving a verbally abusive relationship can be a complex and difficult process. Verbal abuse is a form of emotional abuse that involves the use of words to control, intimidate, or harm a partner. It can take many forms, including name-calling, belittling, threatening, and manipulating. Verbal abuse can be just as damaging as physical abuse, and in some cases, it can be even harder to recognize and leave.

One of the complexities of leaving a verbally abusive relationship is that the abuse may not be obvious to others. Unlike physical abuse, which leaves visible bruises or scars, verbal abuse often goes unseen. This can make it difficult for a victim to get support from friends and family, who may not understand the gravity of the situation. Additionally, many victims of verbal abuse may not even realize that they are in an abusive relationship, as the abuser's words can be so normalized over time.

Another complexity is that verbal abuse can take many forms and can be hard to identify. It can be subtle, such as constant criticism or negative comments, or it can be more overt, such as yelling or threatening. This can make it difficult for a victim to recognize that they are being abused and to identify the specific behaviors that are harmful.

Another complexity is that leaving a verbally abusive relationship can be dangerous. Abusers often use threats and intimidation to control their victims, and they may become violent when a victim tries to leave. Many victims may fear for their safety or the safety of their children, making the decision to leave even more difficult.

Additionally, many victims of verbal abuse may also experience financial abuse, which can make it even harder to leave. Financial abuse can involve controlling a victim's access to money, limiting their ability to work, or using their money without their consent. This can leave a victim without the means to support themselves or their children, making it difficult to leave the abuser.

Moreover, leaving a verbally abusive relationship can be emotionally and mentally challenging. Verbal abuse can take a toll on a person's self-esteem and mental health. Many victims may feel guilty, ashamed, or responsible for the abuse. They may also feel isolated and alone, and may have difficulty trusting others. They may also have difficulty forgiving themselves for staying in the relationship for so long.

Lastly, verbal abuse often continues even after a victim leaves the relationship. Abusers may stalk, harass, or threaten their victims, making it difficult for them to move on and rebuild their lives. This can make leaving a verbally abusive relationship a long-term process that requires on-going support and resources.

In conclusion, leaving a verbally abusive relationship can be a complex and difficult process. It is important for victims to understand that they are not alone, and that there are resources and support available to help them. They should also reach out to friends and family and seek professional help, such as counseling or therapy, to help them cope with the emotional and mental effects of verbal abuse. It is also important for victims to have a safety plan in place before leaving the relationship, and to seek legal assistance if necessary. With the right support and resources, victims can leave an abusive relationship and start to rebuild their lives.

It is important to note that leaving a verbally abusive relationship is not a one-time event, but rather a process. It can take time for a victim to fully understand and recognize the abuse, as well as to build the resources and support necessary to leave. It is also important to understand that leaving an abusive relationship does not necessarily mean that the abuse will stop. Abusers may continue to stalk, harass, or threaten their victims, even after the relationship is over.

One important step in leaving a verbally abusive relationship is to create a safety plan. This can include things like identifying safe places to go, having a trusted person to call in case of an emergency, and having important documents and money hidden in a safe place. It is also important to inform trusted friends and family members of the situation and to seek legal assistance if necessary.

It is also important for victims to seek professional help, such as counseling or therapy. A therapist or counselor can provide emotional and mental support, as well as help a victim understand and cope with the effects of verbal abuse. They can also help a victim work through feelings of guilt, shame, or responsibility, and help them build self-esteem and self-confidence.

Another important step in leaving a verbally abusive relationship is to build a support system. This can include friends, family members, and support groups. Support groups can be especially helpful, as they provide a safe space for victims to share their experiences and connect with others who have been through similar situations.

Finally, it is important for victims to take care of themselves physically, emotionally, and mentally. This can include things like getting enough sleep, eating well, and engaging in regular exercise. It is also important to engage in self-care activities, such as reading a book, listening to music, or taking a relaxing bath.

In conclusion, leaving a verbally abusive relationship is a complex and difficult process. It requires a victim to understand and recognize the abuse, as well as to build the resources and support necessary to leave. It is important for victims to have a safety plan in place, to seek professional help, and to build a support system. It is also important for victims to take care of themselves physically, emotionally, and mentally, as they begin to rebuild their lives.

# 06: Developing a Support System

Developing a support system is an essential part of maintaining mental and emotional well-being. A support system can consist of family, friends, professional counselors, or support groups. It is a network of people who can provide emotional, practical, and moral support during difficult times.

One of the first steps in developing a support system is to identify the types of support you need. This can include emotional support, practical support, and moral support. Emotional support can come in the form of listening and providing comfort, while practical support can include help with daily tasks or financial assistance. Moral support is the encouragement and validation of your beliefs and values.

Once you have identified the types of support you need, it is important to reach out to the people in your life who can provide that support. This can include family members, friends, or professional counselors. It is also important to consider different types of support groups, such as those for specific mental health conditions or life events.

It is also important to remember that not all support has to come from people. Hobbies, exercise, and other forms of self-care can also be a part of your support system. It is important to find activities that bring you joy and relaxation and make time for them in your schedule.

It is also important to remember that your support system may change over time. As you go through different stages of life, your needs may change and the people and activities that once provided support may not be as effective. It is important to regularly reassess your support system and make changes as needed.

It is also important to remember that you are not alone in developing a support system. There are many resources available to help you, including books, online resources, and professional counseling services.

It is important to remember that seeking support is a sign of strength, not weakness. It takes courage to admit that you need help and to reach out to others for support. By building a support system, you are taking an important step towards maintaining your mental and emotional well-being.

In conclusion, Developing a support system is an essential step towards maintaining mental and emotional well-being. It involves identifying the types of support you need, reaching out to people and activities that can provide that support, and regularly reassessing and making changes as needed. Remember to seek support is a sign of strength, and there are many resources available to help you in the process.

In addition to the steps outlined above, it is also important to establish clear boundaries and communicate your needs effectively within your support system. This means setting limits on what you are comfortable with and what you expect from others in terms of support. It also means being honest and direct about your needs, rather than expecting others to read your mind or make assumptions about what you need.

It is also important to practice self-compassion and self-care within your support system. This means being kind and understanding with yourself, rather than criticizing or judging yourself harshly. It also means taking care of your physical, emotional, and mental needs, such as getting enough rest, eating well, and engaging in activities that bring you joy.

Another important aspect of developing a support system is

learning to manage and cope with stress. Stress can come from a variety of sources, including work, relationships, and personal issues, and can have a significant impact on your mental and emotional well-being. It is important to find healthy ways to manage stress, such as through exercise, mindfulness, or professional counseling.

Finally, it is important to remember that a support system is not a one-time fix. It takes ongoing effort and commitment to maintain and strengthen the relationships within your support system. This means regularly reaching out to the people and activities that provide support, and being open to receiving support from others.

In summary, developing a support system is an ongoing process that requires clear communication, self-compassion, stress management, and ongoing effort to maintain and strengthen relationships. By taking the time to develop a support system, you can improve your mental and emotional well-being and have a network of people to rely on during difficult times. Remember, seeking support is a sign of strength and a vital step towards maintaining mental and emotional well-being.

# 07: The Role of Therapy in Healing from Verbal Abuse

Therapy plays a crucial role in healing from verbal abuse. Verbal abuse is a form of emotional abuse that can have serious and long-lasting effects on an individual's mental and emotional well-being. It is characterized by the use of words and language to belittle, demean, and control the victim. The effects of verbal abuse can be just as damaging as physical abuse and can leave individuals feeling isolated, worthless, and hopeless.

The first step in healing from verbal abuse is recognizing that it is happening and that it is not your fault. Verbal abuse is a pattern of behavior used to control and manipulate the victim. It can be difficult to see the abuse for what it is, especially if the abuser is someone you love or trust. A therapist can help you identify the patterns of verbal abuse and understand the dynamics of the relationship.

Once you have identified that you are experiencing verbal abuse, therapy can help you work through the emotions and feelings that come with it. Verbal abuse can leave individuals feeling confused, guilty, and ashamed. It can be difficult to trust yourself and your own perceptions of reality. A therapist can provide a safe and supportive environment for you to process these emotions and work through the trauma.

One of the most important aspects of healing from verbal abuse is learning to set boundaries. Verbal abuse often involves the abuser crossing boundaries and disregarding the victim's needs and wants. Therapy can help you learn how to set and maintain healthy boundaries, both with the abuser and in future relationships. This can help you take control of your life and feel more empowered.

Cognitive Behavioral Therapy (CBT) is one common approach that can be very effective in healing from verbal abuse. CBT is a form of therapy that helps individuals change negative patterns of thinking and behavior. It can help you identify negative thoughts and beliefs that may be keeping you stuck in the cycle of abuse and learn how to challenge and replace them with more positive and healthy thoughts.

Another approach that can be helpful is Eye Movement Desensitization and Reprocessing (EMDR) therapy. EMDR is a form of therapy that uses eye movements or other forms of bilateral stimulation to help individuals process and heal from traumatic events. It has been shown to be effective in treating a wide range of mental health conditions, including those related to verbal abuse.

In addition to individual therapy, group therapy can also be beneficial for those healing from verbal abuse. Group therapy provides the opportunity to connect with others who have experienced similar abuse and gain support and validation. It can also help individuals feel less alone and isolated in their experience.

In conclusion, therapy plays a crucial role in healing from verbal abuse. By recognizing that verbal abuse is happening, working through the emotions and feelings that come with it, setting healthy boundaries, and utilizing effective therapeutic approaches such as CBT and EMDR, individuals can begin to heal and take control of their lives. It is important to seek professional help and support in order to properly heal from verbal abuse.

Another important aspect of healing from verbal abuse is learning how to communicate effectively. Verbal abuse often involves the abuser using words to control and manipulate the victim. In therapy, individuals can learn how to communicate in a healthy and assertive way. This can include learning how to express one's needs and wants clearly, how to set boundaries, and how to respond to verbal abuse in a way that is empowering rather than disempowering.

It is also important to address any self-esteem issues that may have developed as a result of the verbal abuse. Verbal abuse can leave individuals feeling worthless and worthless. A therapist can help individuals work through these issues and develop a more positive self-image.

In addition to therapy, it is important for individuals healing from verbal abuse to engage in self-care activities. This can include things such as exercise, meditation, journaling, and spending time with supportive friends and family. These activities can help individuals reduce stress and tension, and improve overall well-being.

It is also important to note that healing from verbal abuse is a process and it can take time. It is important for individuals to be patient with themselves and not to expect instant results. It is also important to recognize that healing may be a lifelong process, and individuals may need to continue therapy or other forms of support throughout their lives.

## 07: THE ROLE OF THERAPY IN HEALING FROM VERBAL ABUSE

In conclusion, therapy plays a vital role in healing from verbal abuse. It can help individuals recognize the abuse, work through the emotions and feelings that come with it, learn to set healthy boundaries, and communicate effectively. Therapy can also help address self-esteem issues and aid in the development of a positive self-image. Additionally, self-care activities and patience with oneself are important aspects of the healing process. It is important for individuals who have experienced verbal abuse to seek professional help and support in order to properly heal and regain control of their lives.

# 08: Understanding Gaslighting and How to Spot It

Gaslighting is a form of psychological manipulation in which a person or group makes someone question their sanity, memory, or perception of events. It can be incredibly damaging, as it undermines's a person's sense of reality and can lead to feelings of confusion, self-doubt, and even depression. In this chapter, we will discuss the signs of gaslighting, the effects it can have, and what you can do if you suspect someone is gaslighting you.

One of the most common signs of gaslighting is that the person or group doing it will deny or minimise the events that you remember happening. They may tell you that you are imagining things, that you are too sensitive, or that you are overreacting. They may also try to convince you that others, such as friends and family, are lying to you or that they are the only ones who truly understand you.

Another sign of gaslighting is that the person or group will often try to control your behaviour or reactions. They may do this by telling you what to do, how to think, or how to feel. They may also try to isolate you from your support system, such as friends and family, in order to further control your behaviour and reactions.

Gaslighting can also manifest in the form of projecting their own behaviour and actions on to the victim. For example, they may accuse the victim of being the one who is lying, manipulating, or controlling the situation when it is actually the perpetrator who is doing so.

The effects of gaslighting can be severe and long-lasting. People who have been gaslighted may experience feelings of confusion, self-doubt, anxiety, depression, and even paranoia. They may also develop trust issues and have difficulty forming healthy relationships in the future.

If you suspect that someone is gaslighting you, it is important to trust your instincts. Remember that you have a right to your own thoughts, feelings, and experiences, and that no one has the right to make you question them. It is also important to seek support from trusted friends and family, as well as a therapist, who can help you navigate this difficult situation.

It is also important to keep a record of the events and incidents that you believe are gaslighting. This can help you to see patterns and make it easier to communicate your experiences to others.

It is important to understand that gaslighting is a form of emotional abuse, and it is never okay to be treated this way. If you are experiencing gaslighting, it is important to reach out for help, whether it's from a therapist, a friend, or a family member. Remember that you are not alone, and that there are people who care about you and want to support you.

In conclusion, gaslighting is a form of psychological manipulation that can be incredibly damaging. It can make you question your own reality and lead to feelings of confusion, self-doubt, and depression. However, by being aware of the signs of gaslighting, trusting your instincts, and seeking support, you can protect yourself from its harmful effects.

It is also important to note that gaslighting can occur in a variety of settings, including personal relationships, work environments, and even in political or social contexts. In personal relationships, gaslighting can be used by a partner or spouse to control and manipulate their partner. In a work environment, gaslighting can be used by a superior to maintain power and control over their subordinates. In political or social contexts, gaslighting can be used by leaders or groups to manipulate public opinion and maintain control over a population.

It is important to be aware of the different forms that gaslighting can take, and to recognize that it is not limited to just personal relationships. Gaslighting can occur in any setting where power dynamics are present, and it can have serious consequences for both individuals and society as a whole.

Another important aspect of gaslighting is that it is often used in conjunction with other forms of abuse, such as emotional, physical, and sexual abuse. Gaslighting can make it difficult for a victim to recognize and acknowledge other forms of abuse, and it can make it even harder for them to leave or seek help.

It is crucial for victims of gaslighting to not only seek help for themselves but to also educate themselves about the dynamics of gaslighting and abuse. This can help them to better understand what they are experiencing and to make informed decisions about how to move forward.

There are also organizations and resources available to support those who have been affected by gaslighting. These can include hotlines, counseling services, and support groups. It is important to seek out these resources and to not be afraid to reach out for help.

In conclusion, gaslighting is a serious form of psychological manipulation that can have severe and long-lasting effects. It can occur in a variety of settings and often in conjunction with other forms of abuse. It is crucial for individuals to be aware of the signs of gaslighting and to trust their instincts. Seeking support from friends, family, and professionals, as well as education and resources, can help individuals to protect themselves from the harmful effects of gaslighting and to move forward in a healthy and positive way.

# 09: The Cycle of Abuse and How to Break Free

The Cycle of Abuse is a pattern of behavior that is commonly seen in abusive relationships. It is a repetitive pattern of behavior that includes three distinct stages: tension building, explosion or abuse, and the honeymoon phase.

During the tension building stage, the abuser may begin to display small acts of controlling behavior. This can include verbal abuse, threats, or other forms of manipulation. The victim may begin to feel uneasy and on edge during this stage, as they sense that something is about to happen.

The explosion or abuse stage is when the abuser physically or emotionally harms the victim. This stage can include physical violence, emotional manipulation, or verbal abuse. The victim may feel scared and powerless during this stage.

The honeymoon phase is when the abuser may apologize, promise to change, or try to make up for the abuse. The victim may feel relieved and hopeful that the abuser will change their behavior. However, this stage is usually short-lived, and the cycle of abuse begins again.

## 09: THE CYCLE OF ABUSE AND HOW TO BREAK FREE

Breaking the cycle of abuse is a difficult process and takes a lot of work and support. The first step is to recognize that you are in an abusive relationship. Many victims of abuse may not realize that they are being abused, or they may blame themselves for the abuser's behavior.

The next step is to create a safety plan. This includes identifying safe places to go, people to call, and ways to protect yourself. It is also important to have a plan for leaving the relationship if necessary.

Another important step is to seek help from professionals. This can include therapists, counselors, or domestic violence advocates. They can provide support and guidance in dealing with the abuse and healing from it.

It is also important to surround yourself with supportive friends and family who can provide emotional support. They can also help to hold you accountable for ending the relationship.

It is important to remember that breaking the cycle of abuse is a process and it takes time. It is important to be patient with yourself and not to rush into any decisions.

It is also important to remember that leaving an abuser is not a one-time event, but rather a process. It may take multiple attempts to leave before it is successful.

In summary, breaking free from the cycle of abuse is a difficult process, but it is possible. The first step is recognizing that you are in an abusive relationship, creating a safety plan, seeking help from professionals and friends and family, and being patient with yourself. Remember that leaving an abuser is not a one-time event, it may take multiple attempts.

Additionally, it is important to understand that healing from abuse is not a linear process. There may be moments of progress, followed by setbacks and triggers. It is important to be kind and compassionate towards yourself during this process.

It is also important to understand that the abuse is not your fault. Abusive behavior is a choice made by the abuser and they are responsible for their actions. It is not something that you caused or deserved.

Another crucial step in breaking free from the cycle of abuse is to educate yourself about the dynamics of abuse. Understanding how abuse works and the different forms it can take can help you to recognize it in your own relationship and in relationships of those around you.

It is also important to learn about healthy relationships and what they look like. This can serve as a guide for what you should expect in a relationship and can help you to set boundaries and communicate your needs effectively.

It is also important to understand that breaking free from the cycle of abuse is not just about leaving the abuser, but also about healing from the trauma and rebuilding your life. This may include therapy, self-care practices, and support groups.

It is also important to understand that it is not always possible or safe to leave an abusive relationship. In these situations, it is important to have a safety plan in place and to seek help from professionals.

In conclusion, breaking free from the cycle of abuse is a difficult but possible process. It requires recognition of the abuse, planning for safety, seeking help from professionals, surrounding oneself with supportive friends and family, and understanding the dynamics of abuse and healthy relationships. Additionally, healing from the trauma and rebuilding your life is an important aspect of breaking free from the cycle of abuse. Remember to be patient with yourself, understand that the abuse is not your fault and that healing is a process that takes time.

# 10: The Impact of Verbal Abuse on Children and Families

Verbal abuse is a form of emotional abuse that can have devastating effects on children and families. This type of abuse involves the use of words or language to control, manipulate, or belittle another person. It can take many forms, including name-calling, yelling, threatening, and shaming. The effects of verbal abuse can be just as severe as those of physical abuse, leaving long-lasting emotional scars on both children and adults.

Children who are exposed to verbal abuse may experience a wide range of negative effects on their emotional, psychological, and physical well-being. They may develop feelings of low self-worth, self-doubt, and insecurity. They may also experience depression, anxiety, and other mental health issues. Children who are exposed to verbal abuse may also struggle with trust issues and have difficulty forming healthy relationships in the future.

In addition to the emotional effects, children who are exposed to verbal abuse may also experience physical symptoms. These can include headaches, stomachaches, and trouble sleeping. They may also develop behavioral problems, such as aggression, defiant behavior, and difficulties with concentration and memory.

Families affected by verbal abuse can also experience a wide range of negative effects. The constant tension and stress can lead to a breakdown in communication and a lack of trust within the family. Children may also begin to withdraw from their family and may struggle to form healthy relationships with their parents or caregivers.

There are also long-term effects of verbal abuse that can carry on into adulthood. Children who have experienced verbal abuse may grow up to have difficulty trusting others, difficulty forming healthy relationships, and may have a tendency to engage in emotionally abusive behavior themselves. They may also have a higher risk of developing mental health issues such as depression and anxiety.

It is important to understand that verbal abuse is not always obvious. It can be subtle and insidious, making it difficult for both children and adults to recognize. Some common signs of verbal abuse include:

– Name-calling or belittling language

# 10: THE IMPACT OF VERBAL ABUSE ON CHILDREN AND FAMILIES

– Constant criticism or put-downs

– Yelling or screaming

– Threatening language or behavior

– Shaming or embarrassing language or behavior

It is important for parents, caregivers, and other adults who work with children to be aware of the signs of verbal abuse and to take action to protect children from its negative effects. This may include seeking counseling or therapy, either individually or as a family, to work through the effects of verbal abuse and to learn healthy communication and problem-solving skills.

It is also important for adults to model healthy communication and relationships for children. This means avoiding verbal abuse and instead using positive, supportive language and behavior. It is also important to teach children how to recognize and report verbal abuse, both in their own lives and in the lives of others.

In conclusion, verbal abuse is a serious form of emotional abuse that can have devastating effects on children and families. It can lead to a wide range of negative effects on children's emotional, psychological, and physical well-being, as well as on the well-being of families. It is important for adults to be aware of the signs of verbal abuse and to take action to protect children from its negative effects. This may include seeking counseling or therapy, modeling healthy communication and relationships, and teaching children how to recognize and report verbal abuse.

It is crucial for individuals who have been affected by verbal abuse to seek help and support. This can include individual therapy, couples or family therapy, or support groups. Therapy can provide a safe and supportive environment to process the trauma of verbal abuse, work through any lingering effects, and learn how to cope with triggers and flashbacks.

In addition to therapy, it may be beneficial for individuals to educate themselves on the topic of verbal abuse. This can include reading books, articles, or watching documentaries on the topic. It can also include learning about the dynamics of verbal abuse and the different tactics used by abusers. This knowledge can empower individuals to recognize verbal abuse and to understand that they are not to blame for the abuse they have suffered.

For those who are struggling with verbal abuse in their current relationships, it is important to reach out for help and support. This may include talking to a therapist, a trusted friend or family member, or a domestic violence advocate. It may also include leaving the relationship if the abuse is ongoing and the abuser is unwilling to change their behavior. Leaving an abusive relationship can be a difficult and dangerous process, so it is important to have a safety plan in place and to have support from trusted individuals.

Moreover, it is important for society as a whole to recognize verbal abuse as a serious form of emotional abuse. This includes changing the way we talk about verbal abuse and recognizing it as a significant form of abuse. It also means holding abusers accountable for their actions and providing support and resources for survivors of verbal abuse.

In conclusion, verbal abuse can have severe effects on children and families, leaving long-lasting emotional scars. It is important for individuals, families, and society as a whole to recognize the signs of verbal abuse and to take action to protect those affected by it. This may include seeking ther-

apy, educating oneself on the topic, leaving abusive relationships, and holding abusers accountable for their actions. With support and resources, individuals can work
through the effects of verbal abuse and learn to live a
healthy and fulfilling life.

# 11: Navigating the Legal System and Seeking Help

Navigating the legal system can be a daunting and confusing task for many individuals. Whether you are dealing with a criminal charge, a civil dispute, or a family issue, it is important to understand your rights and options and to seek help from qualified professionals. In this chapter, we will discuss some key aspects of the legal system and strategies for seeking help.

One of the most important things to understand about the legal system is that it is divided into two main branches: criminal law and civil law. Criminal law deals with crimes committed against society, such as murder or theft, and is enforced by the government through the criminal justice system. Civil law, on the other hand, deals with disputes between private individuals or organizations and is enforced through the civil justice system.

If you are facing a criminal charge, it is important to understand that you have certain constitutional rights, such as the right to a fair trial and the right to legal representation. If you cannot afford a lawyer, the government will appoint one for you. It is also important to understand the different

stages of a criminal case, such as the arrest, the arraign-
ment, the trial, and the appeals process.

If you are involved in a civil dispute, such as a contract dispute or a personal injury case, it is important to understand
the different types of disputes that can be resolved through
the civil justice system. Some of the most common types of
civil cases include contract disputes, personal injury cases,
and disputes over property ownership.

In either case, whether criminal or civil, it is important to
seek help from qualified professionals, such as lawyers or
legal aid organizations. Lawyers can provide you with advice and representation throughout the legal process, and
legal aid organizations can provide you with information
and assistance if you cannot afford a lawyer.

When seeking help from a lawyer, it is important to find a
lawyer who is experienced in the area of law relevant to
your case. You can find a lawyer by asking friends or family
for recommendations, searching online, or contacting a
local bar association. Once you have found a lawyer, it is important to discuss your case and your goals with the lawyer
and to ask any questions you may have.

If you cannot afford a lawyer, there are legal aid organizations that can help you. Legal aid organizations provide free or low-cost legal services to people who cannot afford a lawyer. These organizations can provide you with information and assistance on a variety of legal issues, including criminal charges, civil disputes, and family issues.

In addition to seeking help from lawyers and legal aid organizations, there are other resources available to help you navigate the legal system. For example, there are self-help centers that provide information and assistance to people who are representing themselves in court. There are also legal clinics and pro bono programs that provide free legal services to low-income individuals.

In summary, navigating the legal system can be a challenging task, but it is important to understand your rights and options and to seek help from qualified professionals. Whether you are dealing with a criminal charge, a civil dispute, or a family issue, it is important to find a lawyer who is experienced in the area of law relevant to your case and to discuss your case and your goals with the lawyer. If you cannot afford a lawyer, legal aid organizations and other resources can provide you with information and assistance.

Another important aspect of navigating the legal system is understanding the different types of legal proceedings. For example, there are court trials, arbitration, mediation, and other forms of alternative dispute resolution (ADR). Court trials are the most common form of legal proceeding and involve a judge or jury making a decision about a case. Arbitration and mediation are forms of ADR that involve a neutral third party helping to resolve a dispute.

It's also important to be aware of the different levels of court and jurisdiction. For example, in the U.S, the federal court system and state court system are separate and have different jurisdiction. If the matter involves a federal law, it would be heard in the federal court system, and if it's a state law, it would be heard in the state court system.

Additionally, it is important to understand the statute of limitations for your case. The statute of limitations is a time limit within which a legal action must be taken. If the statute of limitations has expired, you may no longer be able to take legal action.

## 11: NAVIGATING THE LEGAL SYSTEM AND SEEKING HELP

In addition to understanding the legal system and seeking help from qualified professionals, it is also important to be prepared for court proceedings. This includes gathering and organizing relevant documents, preparing for witness interviews, and understanding the court procedures. It's also important to be aware of the potential outcomes of your case and to have realistic expectations.

Finally, it's important to remember that the legal system is not perfect and can be slow and frustrating. It's important to have patience and to maintain a positive attitude throughout the process.

In conclusion, navigating the legal system can be a challenging task, but it is important to understand your rights and options and to seek help from qualified professionals. It's important to understand the different types of legal proceedings, the different levels of court and jurisdiction, and the statute of limitations. Additionally, it's important to be prepared for court proceedings and to have realistic expectations. Remember to be patient and maintain a positive attitude throughout the process.

# 12: The Importance of Self-Care and Self-Compassion

Self-care and self-compassion are important concepts that are often overlooked in our busy, fast-paced lives. They refer to the actions and attitudes that we take to care for ourselves physically, emotionally, and mentally. When we neglect self-care and self-compassion, we can experience burnout, stress, and depression. On the other hand, when we prioritize these practices, we can experience greater well-being, happiness, and success in all areas of our lives.

Self-care is the practice of taking care of our physical, emotional, and mental well-being. This can include things like getting enough sleep, eating a healthy diet, exercising regularly, and engaging in activities that bring us joy. It also includes taking care of our emotional needs by setting healthy boundaries, practicing self-compassion, and seeking support when needed.

Self-compassion is the practice of treating ourselves with the same kindness, care, and understanding that we would offer to a dear friend. This means being understanding of our mistakes and shortcomings, rather than judging and criticizing ourselves. It also means being compassionate when we are facing difficult situations and emotions, rather than pushing them away or denying them.

When we neglect self-care and self-compassion, we can experience negative consequences. For example, if we are constantly working and neglecting our physical and emotional needs, we can experience burnout. This can manifest as physical symptoms such as fatigue and insomnia, as well as emotional symptoms such as depression and anxiety. Neglecting self-compassion can also lead to feelings of worthlessness and self-doubt, which can make it difficult to achieve our goals and be successful in life.

On the other hand, when we prioritize self-care and self-compassion, we can experience greater well-being and success in all areas of our lives. For example, when we take care of our physical and emotional needs, we have more energy and focus to devote to our work and relationships. When we practice self-compassion, we are more resilient and better able to cope with stress and difficult situations.

In order to practice self-care and self-compassion, it is important to be mindful of our needs and take action to meet them. This can include setting aside time each day to engage in self-care practices, such as exercise, meditation, or journaling. It can also include being mindful of our thoughts and emotions, and practicing self-compassion when we notice ourselves being critical or judgmental towards ourselves.

One way to practice self-compassion is to adopt a kind and understanding inner voice. Instead of criticizing ourselves, we can remind ourselves that we are doing the best we can, and that we are not alone in our struggles. We can also remind ourselves that we deserve compassion and kindness, just like everyone else.

In addition to these practices, it is important to be mindful of the messages that we are receiving from the world around us. We are constantly bombarded with images and messages that tell us we should be perfect, and that we should be able to handle everything on our own. These messages can be harmful, and can contribute to feelings of self-doubt and inadequacy. By being mindful of these messages, and reminding ourselves that they are not accurate or helpful, we can begin to counteract them and cultivate a more compassionate and nurturing inner voice.

In conclusion, self-care and self-compassion are essential

for our well-being and success in life. They allow us to take care of our physical, emotional, and mental needs, and to be kind and understanding towards ourselves when we face challenges and difficult emotions. By making self-care and self-compassion a priority, we can experience greater well-being, happiness, and success in all areas of our lives. It is important to remember that self-care and self-compassion are ongoing practices and require regular attention and effort. It is also important to understand that self-care and self-compassion are not selfish, but rather a form of self-love and self-respect. It is essential to take time for ourselves, to nurture ourselves and to be kind to ourselves. By doing so, we can build resilience, increase our ability to cope with stress, and improve our overall well-being. Remember, the better we take care of ourselves, the better we can take care of others. So, make self-care and self-compassion a regular part of your daily routine and you will see a positive change in your life.

# 13: Rebuilding Self-Esteem and Self-Worth

Rebuilding self-esteem and self-worth can be a difficult and challenging process, but it is possible with the right mindset and strategies.

Self-esteem refers to the way we perceive and value ourselves, while self-worth is the value we place on ourselves as a person. Low self-esteem and self-worth can lead to negative thoughts and behaviors, such as self-doubt, self-criticism, and a lack of motivation.

There are several strategies that can be used to rebuild self-esteem and self-worth. One of the most effective ways is to challenge negative thoughts and beliefs. Negative thoughts and beliefs can be limiting and prevent us from reaching our full potential. By identifying and challenging these thoughts, we can start to replace them with more positive and empowering beliefs.

Another important strategy is to focus on self-care and self-compassion. This includes taking care of our physical, emotional, and mental well-being. This can be done by engaging in regular exercise, eating a healthy diet, getting enough sleep, and taking time to relax and unwind. Additionally, practicing self-compassion can help us to be kinder and more understanding towards ourselves, which can help to improve our self-esteem and self-worth.

Setting and achieving goals can also be an effective way to rebuild self-esteem and self-worth. Setting realistic and achievable goals can help to give us a sense of purpose and accomplishment, which can boost our confidence and self-worth.

It is also important to surround yourself with positive and supportive people. Being around people who are supportive and encouraging can help to improve our self-esteem and self-worth. On the other hand, being around negative and critical people can have the opposite effect and can lead to feelings of low self-esteem and self-worth.

Lastly, it is important to remember that rebuilding self-esteem and self-worth takes time and effort. It is not something that can be achieved overnight. It is a process that involves learning new skills, challenging negative thoughts and beliefs, and making positive changes in our lives. It is important to be patient and persistent in our efforts to rebuild our self-esteem and self-worth.

In conclusion, rebuilding self-esteem and self-worth can be a challenging process, but it is possible with the right mindset and strategies. It is important to challenge negative thoughts and beliefs, focus on self-care and self-compassion, set and achieve goals, surround yourself with positive and supportive people, and be patient and persistent in our efforts. With the right mindset and strategies, it is possible to rebuild our self-esteem and self-worth, and live a happier and more fulfilling life.

Another important aspect of rebuilding self-esteem and self-worth is learning to accept and love ourselves for who we are. This means accepting and embracing our flaws and imperfections, rather than constantly trying to change or hide them. It also means learning to appreciate and value our own unique qualities and strengths.

One way to practice self-acceptance is through mindfulness and meditation. These practices can help us to become more aware of our thoughts and feelings, and to observe them without judgment. This can help us to develop a more compassionate and accepting attitude towards ourselves, which can improve our self-esteem and self-worth.

Another way to practice self-acceptance is through journaling. Writing down our thoughts and feelings can help us to process and understand them better, and can also help us to identify patterns and areas where we need to work on accepting ourselves.

Another effective way to rebuild self-esteem and self-worth is by practicing gratitude. Focusing on the things we are grateful for in our lives can help to shift our focus away from negative thoughts and feelings and towards positive ones. It can also help us to appreciate and value ourselves more.

It is also important to remember that self-esteem and self-worth are not fixed traits. They can change and fluctuate depending on various factors such as our life experiences, relationships, and environment. It is important to be mindful of these factors and to work on maintaining our self-esteem and self-worth on a regular basis.

In addition to these strategies, seeking help from a therapist or counselor can also be beneficial in rebuilding self-esteem and self-worth. A therapist or counselor can help to provide guidance and support in identifying and challenging negative thoughts and beliefs, and in developing a more positive and empowering mindset.

Rebuilding self-esteem and self-worth is a journey that requires time, effort and self-compassion. It's not an easy task but it's worth the effort. Remember that you deserve to have high self-esteem and self-worth, and with the right mindset and strategies, you can achieve it.

In conclusion, rebuilding self-esteem and self-worth is a process that can be achieved by challenging negative thoughts and beliefs, focusing on self-care and self-compassion, setting and achieving goals, surrounding yourself with positive and supportive people, practicing self-acceptance, gratitude, and seeking help when needed. It takes time and effort but it is worth it in the end. You deserve to have high self-esteem and self-worth, and you can achieve it with the right mindset and strategies.

# 14: Setting Boundaries and Communicating Effectively

Setting boundaries and communicating effectively are crucial for maintaining healthy relationships and achieving personal fulfillment.

Boundaries are the limits and rules that individuals set for themselves and expect others to respect. These can be physical, emotional, or mental boundaries, and they are necessary for protecting one's personal space, privacy, and well-being. Setting boundaries allows individuals to assert their needs and wants, and to make clear what is and is not acceptable behavior.

Effective communication, on the other hand, involves being able to express oneself clearly, listen actively, and understand the perspectives of others. It is crucial for building trust and resolving conflicts, and it requires both verbal and nonverbal skills.

One of the key elements of setting boundaries is self-awareness. It is important to know one's own values, needs, and limits in order to communicate them to others. This includes identifying and acknowledging one's own feelings

and emotions, and being able to distinguish between what is
one's own responsibility and what belongs to others.

It is also important to be able to express boundaries clearly
and assertively. This means being able to say "no" when necessary and to stand up for oneself without being aggressive
or defensive. It also means being able to set limits and consequences for others who do not respect one's boundaries.

Effective communication, on the other hand, involves being
able to express oneself clearly and actively listening to the
perspectives of others. To communicate effectively, it is important to use "I" statements rather than "you" statements
to express one's own feelings and needs. This allows for a
more productive conversation, as it avoids blame and defensiveness.

Another important aspect of effective communication is active listening. This means paying attention to what the other
person is saying and trying to understand their perspective.
It also means responding with empathy and validation,
rather than interrupting or dismissing their feelings.

Effective communication also requires the ability to compromise and negotiate. This means being willing to find a middle ground and to find solutions that meet the needs of all parties involved.

In order to communicate effectively, it is also important to be aware of nonverbal cues. This includes body language, tone of voice, and facial expressions. These cues can convey just as much, if not more, than the words spoken.

Setting boundaries and communicating effectively is not always easy, but it is essential for maintaining healthy relationships and achieving personal fulfillment. It requires self-awareness, assertiveness, active listening, and the ability to compromise and negotiate. With practice, individuals can learn to set and communicate their boundaries effectively, leading to more fulfilling and healthier relationships.

In conclusion, setting boundaries and communicating effectively are crucial for maintaining healthy relationships and achieving personal fulfillment. It is important to be aware of one's own values, needs, and limits, and to be able to express them clearly and assertively. Additionally, it is important to be able to actively listen and understand the perspectives of others, and to be able to compromise and negotiate. With practice, individuals can learn to set and communicate their boundaries effectively, leading to more fulfilling and healthier relationships.

Another important aspect of setting boundaries is learning how to handle difficult people. Sometimes, people may push our boundaries and try to control or manipulate us. It is important to recognize when this is happening and to know how to respond appropriately. This may involve setting firm limits and consequences, seeking support from others, and learning how to detach emotionally from the situation.

It is also important to remember that boundaries and communication are not one-time events, but ongoing processes. As individuals and relationships change, boundaries may need to be adjusted and communication methods may need to be adapted. It is important to regularly check in with oneself and with others to ensure that boundaries are being respected and that communication is effective.

When setting boundaries, it is important to remember that it is not about controlling or manipulating others, but rather about taking care of oneself and one's own needs. Setting boundaries is not about being selfish, but rather about being self-respecting. It allows individuals to create healthy and fulfilling relationships and to live a more authentic and fulfilling life.

In conclusion, setting boundaries and communicating effectively are essential for maintaining healthy relationships and achieving personal fulfillment. It requires self-awareness, assertiveness, active listening, and the ability to compromise and negotiate. Additionally, it is important to learn how to handle difficult people, and to remember that boundaries and communication are ongoing processes that require regular check-ins. With practice, individuals can learn to set and communicate their boundaries effectively, leading to more fulfilling and healthier relationships.

# 15: Understanding the Abuser and the Abuse

Understanding the abuser and the abuse is crucial in order to effectively address and prevent domestic violence. An abuser is someone who uses physical, emotional, psychological, or sexual abuse to control and manipulate their partner. This can take many forms, including physical violence, intimidation, isolation, economic control, and verbal and emotional abuse.

The abuser's behavior is not random or unpredictable, but rather is a pattern of intentional actions aimed at gaining and maintaining power and control over their partner. The abuser may also have a history of past abuse, either as a victim or perpetrator, and may have a personality disorder such as narcissism or sociopathy.

The abuse itself can have severe and long-lasting effects on the victim, including physical injuries, emotional trauma, and financial insecurity. The victim may also experience feelings of fear, guilt, shame, and isolation. The abuse can also have a negative impact on the victim's children, who may witness the abuse and suffer from its effects.

## 15: UNDERSTANDING THE ABUSER AND THE ABUSE

The abuser's behavior is not the fault of the victim, and the victim should not be blamed for the abuser's actions. It is important to understand that the abuser is responsible for their own behavior, and that the victim is not to blame. The abuser's behavior can be changed through therapy and other forms of intervention, but it takes time and effort.

It is important to understand that abuse is not limited to physical violence, but can take many forms, including emotional, psychological, and sexual abuse. Emotional abuse can include verbal abuse, name-calling, manipulation, and isolation. Psychological abuse can include manipulating and controlling the victim's thoughts and behaviors, and can also include gaslighting, where the abuser manipulates the victim into doubting their own reality.

It is also important to understand that domestic violence can happen to anyone, regardless of race, ethnicity, socioeconomic status, sexual orientation, or gender identity. Anyone can be a victim of abuse, and anyone can be an abuser.

To help victims of abuse, it is important to provide them with a supportive and safe environment, and to connect them with resources such as shelters, counseling, and legal assistance. It is also important to educate the community about domestic violence, and to promote healthy relationships.

In conclusion, understanding the abuser and the abuse is crucial in addressing and preventing domestic violence. Abusers use various forms of abuse to control and manipulate their partners, and their behavior is not the fault of the victim. The effects of the abuse can be severe and long-lasting, and it is important to provide victims with support and resources. Education and community awareness are also important in preventing domestic violence and promoting healthy relationships.

It is also important to note that while the majority of domestic violence victims are women, men can also be victims of abuse. Men may face additional barriers in seeking help, such as societal stereotypes that men should be able to "handle" or "fix" the abuse, or fear of being perceived as weak or unmanly. It is important to acknowledge that domestic violence can happen to anyone and to provide support and resources for male victims as well.

Additionally, it is important to recognize the intersectionality of domestic violence. Individuals who identify as part of marginalized communities, such as people of color, LGBTQ+ individuals, and individuals with disabilities, may face additional barriers in accessing help and support. For example, a person who identifies as LGBTQ+ may not feel comfortable seeking help from organizations or individuals who hold discriminatory views towards their identity. It is crucial to ensure that domestic violence services and resources are inclusive and accessible to all individuals.

Another important aspect of understanding the abuser is recognizing the cycle of abuse. The cycle of abuse is a pattern of behavior that often occurs in abusive relationships, and can include the following stages: tension building, incident, honeymoon, and calm. During the tension building stage, the abuser may become increasingly agitated and the victim may feel on edge. The incident stage is when the abuse occurs, and can include physical, emotional, psychological, or sexual abuse. The honeymoon stage is when the abuser may apologize, make promises to change, and try to make the relationship seem better. The calm stage is when things may seem normal or peaceful again, but the tension and threat of abuse are always present. Recognizing this cycle can help victims understand that the abuse is not their fault and that it is likely to happen again.

It is also important to note that abuser does not only happen in romantic relationships, but also in other relationships such as in families, friends, and workplaces. In these situations, the abuser may use similar tactics of control and manipulation to maintain power and control over the victim.

In order to effectively address and prevent domestic violence, it is crucial to understand the abuser, the abuse, and the impact it has on the victim. This includes recognizing the various forms of abuse, acknowledging that anyone can be a victim or an abuser, and understanding the barriers that marginalized communities may face in accessing help and support. It is also important to recognize the cycle of abuse and the role it plays in abusive relationships. By understanding these dynamics, we can better support victims and hold abusers accountable for their actions.

# 16: The Role of Forgiveness in Healing

Forgiveness is a powerful tool in the healing process. It allows individuals to let go of negative emotions and resentment towards others, and can lead to a greater sense of inner peace and well-being. The act of forgiveness can also improve relationships and lead to greater understanding and empathy.

One of the most important aspects of forgiveness is that it is not about forgetting or excusing harmful behavior. Rather, it is about acknowledging the hurt that has been caused and choosing to let go of the anger and resentment that can consume an individual. This can be a difficult process, and may take time, but it is an important step in the healing process.

Forgiveness can also have a positive impact on physical health. Studies have shown that holding onto resentment and anger can lead to a number of negative health effects, including high blood pressure, heart disease, and weakened immune systems. On the other hand, the act of forgiveness can lead to a decrease in stress and an improvement in overall physical health.

Forgiveness can also play a role in improving relationships. When individuals forgive, they are able to let go of negative feelings towards others and can better understand and empathize with their actions. This can lead to greater communication and understanding, and can ultimately improve relationships.

In addition, forgiveness can also be used as a tool for self-healing. It is not always possible to forgive others, but it is possible to forgive oneself. Self-forgiveness can help individuals to let go of guilt and shame, and can lead to a greater sense of self-worth and self-acceptance.

It is important to note that forgiveness is a personal choice and not everyone may be ready or willing to forgive. It is also not necessary to continue a relationship with someone who has hurt you, and you may still choose to distance yourself from that person.

In conclusion, forgiveness is a powerful tool in the healing process. It allows individuals to let go of negative emotions and resentment towards others, and can lead to a greater sense of inner peace and well-being. The act of forgiveness can also improve relationships and lead to greater understanding and empathy. It is not always easy, but it is a necessary step in the journey towards healing and growth.

Forgiveness is a process, and it may take time to work through the feelings of hurt, anger, and resentment. It is important to allow yourself time to grieve and process the emotions that come with being hurt by someone. It is also important to have a support system in place, whether it be friends, family, or a therapist, to help you work through the process of forgiveness.

It may also be helpful to practice self-care and mindfulness during this process. Engaging in activities such as yoga, meditation, or journaling can help to reduce stress and improve overall well-being. Practicing self-compassion can also be beneficial in the process of forgiveness, as it can help to ease feelings of guilt and shame and promote self-acceptance.

Forgiveness can be challenging, but it is a crucial aspect of the healing process. It is important to remember that forgiveness is not about excusing or forgetting harmful behavior, but rather about acknowledging the hurt that has been caused and choosing to let go of the anger and resentment that can consume an individual.

It is also important to remember that forgiveness is a personal choice and it is not always possible or necessary to forgive others. Some situations may be too hurtful or damaging to forgive, and it is important to respect and honor your own feelings and boundaries.

In summary, forgiveness is a powerful tool in the healing process. It allows individuals to let go of negative emotions and resentment towards others, and can lead to a greater sense of inner peace and well-being. The act of forgiveness can also improve relationships and lead to greater understanding and empathy. It is a process that may take time and may require the help of a support system, self-care, and mindfulness. Remember that forgiveness is a personal choice and should be respected and honored.

# 17: Moving On and Creating a New Life

Moving on from a difficult period in life can be challenging, but it is also an opportunity to create a new and better life. The key to moving forward is to focus on the present and the future, rather than dwelling on the past.

One important step in moving on is to let go of past regrets and mistakes. It is natural to feel remorse or guilt about things that have happened in the past, but dwelling on these feelings will only hold you back from moving forward. Instead, try to learn from your mistakes and make a plan to avoid repeating them in the future.

Another important step in moving on is to focus on your goals and aspirations. Having a clear sense of what you want to achieve in life can give you the motivation and direction you need to move forward. This can be something as simple as setting a daily or weekly task to work towards your goals.

Creating a new life for yourself also involves finding new activities and hobbies to enjoy. This can help to take your mind off of the past and give you a sense of purpose and fulfillment. Try new things and find things that you enjoy doing and that make you feel good.

It's also important to surround yourself with positive and supportive people. Being around people who care about you and encourage you to move forward can make a big difference in your ability to heal and move on.

Another important aspect of moving on and creating a new life is to practice self-care. This includes taking care of your physical, emotional and mental well-being. Eating well, getting enough sleep, and exercising regularly are all important for maintaining good health. Additionally, practicing mindfulness and meditation can help to reduce stress and improve your overall well-being.

Finally, it is important to remember that moving on and creating a new life takes time and effort. It is not something that happens overnight. Be patient with yourself and remember that progress takes time. Celebrate small victories and take one step at a time.

In conclusion, moving on from a difficult period in life can be a challenging but ultimately rewarding process. It involves letting go of past regrets and mistakes, focusing on your goals and aspirations, finding new activities and hobbies, surrounding yourself with positive and supportive people, practicing self-care and being patient with yourself. With dedication and perseverance, anyone can create a new and better life for themselves.

It is also important to remember that it is okay to seek help if needed. Moving on and creating a new life can be difficult, and sometimes it can be hard to do it alone. It is important to seek out professional help if needed. Whether it be a therapist, counselor, or life coach, they can provide you with the support and guidance you need to navigate the process of moving on and creating a new life.

Another way to move on and create a new life is to change your environment. Sometimes, the physical place you are in can hold negative memories or associations that make it hard to move on. If this is the case, consider relocating to a new place. This can be a big step, but it can also be incredibly liberating and give you a fresh start.

Additionally, it can be helpful to focus on gratitude and find things to be thankful for in your life. This can help to shift your focus away from negative experiences and towards the positive things in your life. It can also help to improve your overall outlook and mindset.

Finally, it is important to remember that moving on and creating a new life is a journey, not a destination. It is not something that you will ever fully "finish", but it is a continuous process of growth and self-discovery. Remember to be kind to yourself and take things one step at a time.

In conclusion, moving on and creating a new life is a challenging but ultimately rewarding process. It involves letting go of past regrets and mistakes, focusing on your goals and aspirations, finding new activities and hobbies, surrounding yourself with positive and supportive people, practicing self-care, being patient with yourself, seeking help if needed, changing your environment, focusing on gratitude and remembering that it's a journey. With dedication and perseverance, anyone can move on and create a new and better life for themselves.

# 18: Conclusion: Hope and Healing for Survivors of Verbally Abusive Relationships

Conclusion: Hope and Healing for Survivors of Verbally Abusive Relationships

Verbal abuse is a form of domestic violence that can have a devastating impact on the mental and emotional well-being of its survivors. The constant criticism, belittling, and manipulation can leave individuals feeling worthless, hopeless, and alone. However, it is important for survivors to know that there is hope for healing and recovery.

The first step in the healing process is recognizing that you are in an abusive relationship. This can be difficult as verbal abuse is often subtle and insidious. It can be easy to dismiss the behavior as normal or to blame yourself for the abuse. However, it is important to remember that no one deserves to be treated poorly and that the abuse is not your fault.

Once you have recognized that you are in an abusive relationship, it is important to take steps to protect yourself. This can include setting boundaries, seeking out support from friends and family, and seeking professional help. It is also important to have a plan in place in case of an emergency, such as a safe place to go or a way to contact someone for help.

In addition to taking steps to protect yourself, it is also important to begin the process of healing. This can include therapy, counseling, or support groups. These resources can provide a safe space for survivors to process their experiences and learn coping mechanisms for dealing with the emotional trauma of verbal abuse.

It is also important to focus on self-care and self-compassion. Survivors of verbal abuse may have a tendency to blame themselves or to internalize the negative messages they have been told. It is important to remind yourself that you are not responsible for the abuse and that you deserve to be treated with kindness and respect. Self-care practices such as exercise, meditation, and journaling can be helpful in rebuilding self-esteem and promoting healing.

Recovering from a verbally abusive relationship can be a long and difficult process, but it is possible. With the right support, survivors can learn to move past the trauma of their experiences and build a happier and healthier life for themselves.

It's important to remember that healing is not a linear process and it may take time. It's also important to note that healing may not involve reconciliation or returning to the relationship, Sometimes the best decision is to move on and leave the relationship behind.

Remember that healing is a personal journey, and what works for one person may not work for another. It's important to find what works for you and to be patient with yourself. It's also important to remember that healing is not about forgetting the past, but about learning to live with it in a healthy way.

In conclusion, survivors of verbal abuse can find hope and healing through recognizing the abuse, taking steps to protect themselves, seeking professional help, focusing on self-care and self-compassion, and remembering that healing is a personal journey. It's important to remember that healing is possible and that you deserve to live a happy and healthy life.

Another important aspect of healing is learning to recognize and challenge negative thought patterns that may have been instilled by the abuser. Verbal abusers often use manipulation and gaslighting to make their victims question their own perception of reality and doubt their own abilities. As a result, survivors may struggle with feelings of self-doubt, guilt, and insecurity.

It is important for survivors to learn how to recognize and challenge these negative thought patterns. This can be done through cognitive-behavioral therapy, which can help individuals identify and change negative thoughts and beliefs. It can also be helpful to seek out positive role models and surround yourself with supportive people who can help you rebuild your self-esteem and confidence.

It is also important for survivors to understand that healing is not about going back to the way things were before the abuse. It is about creating a new and better life for yourself. This may involve making changes in your life such as leaving the abuser, finding a new job, or moving to a new place. It may also involve setting new goals and working towards achieving them.

Another important aspect of healing is learning how to cope

with triggers and flashbacks. These can be triggered by certain events, places, or people, and can cause survivors to relive the traumatic experiences of the abuse. It is important for survivors to develop coping mechanisms for dealing with triggers and flashbacks, such as deep breathing, meditation, or journaling.

Finally, it is important for survivors to understand that healing is not a one-time event, but a ongoing process. There will be good days and bad days, and it is important to be patient with yourself and to continue to seek out support when needed. It is also important to remember that healing is not about perfection, but about progress. Every small step forward is a step in the right direction.

In conclusion, hope and healing are possible for survivors of verbally abusive relationships. It is important to recognize the abuse, take steps to protect yourself, seek professional help, focus on self-care and self-compassion, challenge negative thought patterns, make changes in your life, develop coping mechanisms for triggers, and understand that healing is a ongoing process. Remember to be patient with yourself and to continue to seek out support as you move for-

## 18: CONCLUSION: HOPE AND HEALING FOR SURVIVORS OF VERBALLY ABUSIVE RELATIONSHIPS

ward in your journey towards healing.

# Book 3 - Empower Yourself

A Comprehensive Guide to Unlocking Your Inner Potential and Achieving Success in Every Area of Your Life Through Self-Discovery, Personal Development, and Mindset Mastery

# 01: Introduction: Unlocking Your Inner Potential

Introduction

We all have the potential to achieve great things, but sometimes it can be difficult to tap into that potential. Whether it's due to self-doubt, fear, or a lack of understanding of our own abilities, unlocking our inner potential can seem like a daunting task. But the truth is, it's not as difficult as we may think. With the right mindset and a few key strategies, anyone can unlock their inner potential and achieve their goals.

First, it's important to understand that our potential is not fixed. We are not limited by our past experiences or our current circumstances. Instead, our potential is constantly evolving and expanding as we learn new things and develop new skills. This means that we have the ability to improve and grow, no matter how old we are or what we've accomplished so far.

One of the key ways to unlock our inner potential is to set clear, specific goals. This means taking the time to think about what we want to achieve, and then breaking that goal down into smaller, actionable steps. This not only helps us to focus our efforts, but it also gives us a sense of direction and purpose, which can be incredibly motivating.

Another important strategy for unlocking our inner potential is to focus on our strengths. We all have unique talents and abilities, and focusing on these strengths can help us to achieve our goals more easily and efficiently. This means taking the time to identify our strengths and then finding ways to use them in our everyday lives, whether that's at work, at home, or in our personal relationships.

Another key strategy for unlocking our inner potential is to be proactive. This means taking control of our own lives and taking steps to achieve our goals, rather than waiting for opportunities to come to us. Being proactive also means being willing to take risks and step out of our comfort zones. It's easy to get stuck in a rut, but taking risks and trying new things can help us to discover new opportunities and unlock our inner potential.

It's also important to build a supportive network of people around us. Whether it's friends, family, or colleagues, having people in our lives who believe in us and support our goals can make a huge difference in our ability to achieve them. These people can provide guidance, encouragement, and a sounding board for our ideas and aspirations.

Finally, one of the most important strategies for unlocking our inner potential is to be open to learning and growth. This means being willing to try new things, make mistakes, and learn from our experiences. We are never done learning and growing, and by embracing this mindset, we can continue to unlock our inner potential and achieve our goals.

In conclusion, unlocking our inner potential is not as difficult as we may think. It's about setting clear, specific goals, focusing on our strengths, being proactive, building a supportive network, and being open to learning and growth. By following these strategies, we can tap into our inner potential and achieve the things we've always dreamed of.

Another important aspect of unlocking our inner potential is self-awareness. Understanding who we are, what motivates us, and what our values and beliefs are is crucial in order to set meaningful and achievable goals. Self-awareness also allows us to identify and overcome limiting beliefs and negative self-talk that may be holding us back.

# 01: INTRODUCTION: UNLOCKING YOUR INNER PO-TENTIAL

One way to increase self-awareness is through mindfulness practices such as meditation or journaling. These practices can help us to quiet the constant chatter of our minds and tune into our inner selves. This can also give us a deeper understanding of our thoughts, feelings, and behaviors and how they may be impacting our ability to reach our potential.

Another way to increase self-awareness is to seek feedback from others. This could be through a mentor, coach or even a trusted friend or family member. This can provide valuable perspective and insights on areas where we may be holding ourselves back and areas where we excel.

In addition to self-awareness, another important aspect of unlocking our inner potential is self-care. Taking care of our physical, emotional, and mental well-being is crucial in order to be able to perform at our best. This means making sure we are getting enough sleep, eating a healthy diet, and exercising regularly. It also means taking the time to do things that bring us joy and make us feel good, such as spending time with loved ones, reading, or pursuing a hobby.

# 01: INTRODUCTION: UNLOCKING YOUR INNER PO-
# TENTIAL

Self-care also means setting boundaries and learning to say no when necessary. Taking on too much can lead to burnout, and this can have a negative impact on our ability to reach our potential. Learning to say no to things that don't align with our values and goals can free up time and energy to focus on the things that truly matter to us.

In conclusion, unlocking our inner potential is a journey that requires self-awareness, self-care, and the right mindset. By setting clear, specific goals, focusing on our strengths, being proactive, building a supportive network, and being open to learning and growth. By being mindful and taking care of ourselves, and seeking feedback from others, we can tap into our inner potential and achieve the things we've always dreamed of. Remember, unlocking our inner potential is not a one-time event, it's a lifelong process. Keep an open mind, be patient with yourself and enjoy the journey.

# 02: The Power of Self-Discovery

The Power of Self-Discovery

Self-discovery is the process of uncovering one's true self, understanding one's strengths and weaknesses, and recognizing one's deepest desires and values. It is a journey of self-exploration that leads to personal growth and fulfillment. The power of self-discovery lies in its ability to empower individuals to take control of their lives and create the reality they desire.

The first step in the process of self-discovery is to look within oneself. This means examining one's thoughts, emotions, and behavior patterns. It is important to be honest with oneself and to acknowledge any negative thoughts or behaviors that may be holding one back. This can be difficult and uncomfortable, but it is essential for personal growth.

Once one has a better understanding of their thoughts and behaviors, the next step is to identify one's values and beliefs. Values are the principles that guide our actions and shape our worldview. They can include things like integrity, honesty, and compassion. Beliefs, on the other hand, are the assumptions and convictions we hold about ourselves and the world around us. It is important to be aware of our values and beliefs as they shape our actions and reactions to the world around us.

As one continues on their journey of self-discovery, it is important to set goals and create a plan of action. This means identifying the areas of one's life that they would like to improve, setting specific and measurable goals, and creating a plan of action to achieve those goals. This can include things like learning a new skill, starting a new hobby, or making changes to one's career.

One of the most powerful aspects of self-discovery is the ability to understand and accept one's true self. This means being comfortable with one's strengths and weaknesses and accepting oneself for who they are. It also means being open to change and growth, while still being true to oneself.

Self-discovery also involves recognizing and understanding one's deepest desires and passions. This means identifying what truly brings one joy and fulfillment, and making the conscious decision to pursue those things. This can be difficult, as it may involve taking risks and stepping outside of one's comfort zone, but it is essential for achieving true happiness and fulfillment.

Self-discovery also involves being mindful of one's relationships and interactions with others. This means being aware of how one's actions and words affect others and making conscious decisions to improve those interactions. It also means building strong and supportive relationships with others and learning to communicate effectively.

In conclusion, the power of self-discovery lies in its ability to empower individuals to take control of their lives and create the reality they desire. It involves looking within oneself, identifying one's values and beliefs, setting goals and creating a plan of action, understanding and accepting one's true self, recognizing one's deepest desires and passions, and being mindful of one's relationships and interactions with others. It is a journey that can lead to personal growth and fulfillment.

Self-discovery is a continuous process, and it is important to make time to reflect and evaluate one's progress regularly. Remember that self-discovery is not about perfection, it is about growth, and you will make mistakes, but that is okay, it is a part of the process. Keep an open mind, be patient with yourself, and don't be afraid to seek help or guidance if you need it. Remember that the power of self-discovery is within you and that you have the ability to create the life you desire.

Another important aspect of self-discovery is learning to let go of limiting beliefs and negative self-talk. These are the thoughts and beliefs that hold us back and prevent us from reaching our full potential. Examples of limiting beliefs include "I'm not good enough," "I'll never be successful," or "I can't do that." These beliefs can be deeply ingrained and can take time and effort to overcome.

One way to start changing limiting beliefs is to challenge them. Ask yourself where these beliefs came from and if they are truly accurate. It can also be helpful to reframe these beliefs in a more positive light. For example, instead of saying "I'm not good enough," try saying "I am constantly improving and working towards my goals."

It is also important to practice self-compassion during the process of self-discovery. This means being kind and understanding towards oneself, instead of being overly critical. Self-compassion involves recognizing that everyone makes mistakes and has flaws, and that it is normal to have negative thoughts and feelings. It also means treating oneself with the same kindness and understanding that one would offer to a friend.

Another important aspect of self-discovery is learning to take responsibility for one's actions and decisions. This means recognizing that one is in control of their own life and that they have the power to make changes. It also means being accountable for the consequences of one's actions and taking responsibility for the outcomes.

In addition to the above, Self-discovery also includes understanding and exploring one's cultural, ethnic, and social identity. This includes understanding one's own history and heritage and how that shapes one's perspective, values and beliefs. It also includes understanding the different cultural and social groups one belongs to and how those groups shape one's experiences and interactions with the world.

In conclusion, self-discovery is a continuous journey of personal growth and fulfillment. It involves looking within oneself, identifying one's values and beliefs, setting goals and creating a plan of action, understanding and accepting one's true self, recognizing one's deepest desires and passions, being mindful of one's relationships and interactions with others, let go of limiting beliefs and negative self-talk, practicing self-compassion and taking responsibility for one's actions, and understanding and exploring one's cultural, ethnic, and social identity. It is a powerful tool that can empower individuals to create the life they desire. Remember to be patient and kind to yourself, and don't be afraid to seek help and guidance when needed.

# 03: Setting and Achieving Goals

Setting and achieving goals is an essential part of personal and professional growth and development. Goals provide direction and motivation, helping us to focus our efforts and resources towards something specific and meaningful. But goal-setting is not always easy. In order to set and achieve goals that are truly meaningful and effective, it is important to understand the key principles and practices of goal-setting.

The first step in setting and achieving goals is to identify what you truly want. This may seem like an obvious step, but it is one that is often overlooked or rushed through. To identify what you truly want, you need to take the time to reflect on your values, passions, and aspirations. This will help you to identify what is truly important to you, and to set goals that are aligned with your values and passions.

Once you have identified what you truly want, the next step is to set specific, measurable, and achievable goals. Specific goals are those that are clear and specific, stating exactly what you want to achieve. Measurable goals are those that can be quantified and tracked, so that you can measure your progress and know when you have achieved your goal.

## 03: SETTING AND ACHIEVING GOALS

Achievable goals are those that are realistic and attainable, taking into account your current resources and circumstances.

In addition to setting specific, measurable, and achievable goals, it is also important to set goals that are time-bound. This means setting a deadline for when you want to achieve your goal. Having a deadline helps to create a sense of urgency and gives you a clear target to work towards. It also helps to keep you motivated and on track, as you can see the progress you are making towards your goal.

Once you have set your goals, the next step is to create a plan of action. This means breaking down your goals into smaller, manageable tasks and steps. This will help you to focus your efforts and resources, and to make steady progress towards your goal. It is also important to set milestones along the way, so that you can track your progress and adjust your plan as needed.

As you work towards your goals, it is important to stay motivated and focused. This can be challenging, especially when faced with obstacles or setbacks. One way to stay motivated is to remind yourself of why your goal is important to you, and to remind yourself of the benefits and rewards that you will gain by achieving your goal.

Another way to stay motivated is to surround yourself with positive and supportive people. This includes friends, family, and colleagues who will support and encourage you in your efforts to achieve your goals. It is also important to seek out mentors and role models who can provide guidance and inspiration.

Finally, it is important to celebrate your successes and to learn from your mistakes. When you achieve a goal, take the time to celebrate and acknowledge your accomplishment. This will help to boost your confidence and motivation, and will give you a sense of accomplishment and satisfaction. When you encounter obstacles or setbacks, take the time to reflect on what went wrong and to learn from your mistakes. This will help you to make adjustments and to improve your performance in the future.

In conclusion, setting and achieving goals is an essential part of personal and professional growth and development. It is important to identify what you truly want, to set specific, measurable, and achievable goals that are time-bound, to create a plan of action, to stay motivated and focused, to surround yourself with positive and supportive people, and to celebrate your successes and learn from your mistakes. By following these principles and practices, you can set and achieve goals that are truly meaningful and effective, and that will help you to achieve your full potential in life.

Another important aspect of goal setting is to be accountable for your actions. This means taking responsibility for your goals and being accountable for the steps you take to achieve them. This includes setting up a system for tracking your progress, such as a journal or spreadsheet, and regularly reviewing your progress to ensure you are on track. It also means being open to feedback and taking responsibility for any mistakes or setbacks you encounter along the way.

Another key aspect of goal setting is to be flexible and adaptable. This means being willing to change course or adjust your plans as needed. Sometimes, unforeseen circumstances or new information may arise that require you to change your approach. Being open to change and willing to adapt your plans will help you to stay on track and achieve your goals.

Additionally, it's important to have a positive attitude when working towards your goals. Having a positive mindset can help you to stay motivated, overcome obstacles, and believe in yourself. If you find yourself struggling to maintain a positive attitude, consider incorporating mindfulness practices like meditation or yoga into your daily routine.

Lastly, it's crucial to set goals that are challenging but not overwhelming. Setting goals that are too easy or unrealistic can lead to a lack of motivation and a lack of progress. On the other hand, setting goals that are too difficult can lead to frustration and burnout. It's important to find a balance that pushes you to grow and develop, but also allows you to maintain a healthy work-life balance.

In summary, setting and achieving goals is an essential part of personal and professional growth and development. It requires identifying what you truly want, setting specific, measurable, and achievable goals, creating a plan of action, staying motivated, surrounding yourself with positive and supportive people, celebrating your successes, learning from your mistakes, being accountable, being adaptable, having a positive attitude and setting challenging but not overwhelming goals. By following these principles and prac-

tices, you can set and achieve goals that are truly meaningful and effective, and that will help you to achieve your full
potential in life.

# 04: Overcoming Limiting Beliefs

Limiting beliefs are thoughts or ideas that we hold about ourselves that limit our potential and prevent us from reaching our goals. These beliefs can be deeply ingrained in our minds, and can be difficult to overcome. However, by understanding the nature of limiting beliefs and taking steps to challenge and replace them, we can break free from their hold and achieve greater success and fulfillment in our lives.

One of the first steps in overcoming limiting beliefs is to identify them. This can be difficult, as limiting beliefs are often subconscious and may not be immediately obvious. However, by paying attention to our thoughts and feelings, we can begin to notice patterns and themes that indicate the presence of limiting beliefs. For example, if we find ourselves consistently saying things like "I can't do that," "I'm not good enough," or "I'm not smart enough," these may be indicators of limiting beliefs.

Once we have identified our limiting beliefs, we can begin to challenge them. This can be done by asking ourselves questions such as: "Is this belief really true?" "Where did this belief come from?" "What evidence do I have to support this belief?" By questioning the validity of our limiting beliefs, we can begin to see them for what they are: self-imposed limitations that are not based on reality.

Another important step in overcoming limiting beliefs is to replace them with more empowering beliefs. This can be done by identifying the opposite of our limiting belief, and actively working to adopt that belief instead. For example, if our limiting belief is "I can't do that," we can replace it with the belief "I can do anything I set my mind to." By replacing our limiting beliefs with positive, empowering beliefs, we can shift our mindset and open ourselves up to new possibilities.

It's also important to remember that limiting beliefs are often based on past experiences, and that we are not defined by these experiences. We can learn from our past, but we do not have to be limited by it. We can choose to let go of past experiences and move forward, focusing on the present and the future.

In addition, it's helpful to surround ourselves with supportive people who believe in us and our abilities. This can be family, friends, or even a therapist or coach. Having people around us who believe in us and support us can help us to believe in ourselves and overcome our limiting beliefs.

It's also important to be kind to ourselves and practice self-compassion. Beating ourselves up and criticizing ourselves only reinforces limiting beliefs. Instead, we should try to be kind and understanding with ourselves, and acknowledge that we're all human and we all make mistakes.

Finally, practice visualization and affirmations. Visualizing ourselves achieving our goals and using affirmations can help us to overcome limiting beliefs by reinforcing positive thoughts and beliefs in our minds.

In conclusion, overcoming limiting beliefs is not easy, but it is possible. By identifying and challenging our limiting beliefs, replacing them with more empowering beliefs, and surrounding ourselves with supportive people, we can break free from the hold of limiting beliefs and achieve greater success and fulfillment in our lives. Remember to be kind to yourself, practice visualization, and affirmations.

Another powerful tool for overcoming limiting beliefs is mindfulness. Mindfulness is the practice of being present and fully engaged in the current moment, without judgment. When we are mindful, we can observe our thoughts and feelings without getting caught up in them. This allows us to gain perspective on our limiting beliefs and see them for what they are: just thoughts, not necessarily reality.

Mindfulness can be practiced through various techniques such as meditation, yoga, or simply taking a few deep breaths and focusing on the present moment. By incorporating mindfulness into our daily lives, we can learn to observe our thoughts and feelings without getting caught up in them, and gain a deeper understanding of the nature of our limiting beliefs.

Another effective strategy for overcoming limiting beliefs is to take action. Often, limiting beliefs stem from fear of failure or rejection. By taking small, manageable steps towards our goals, we can begin to challenge these fears and build confidence in our abilities. As we begin to see that we can accomplish what we set out to do, our limiting beliefs will lose their power over us.

It's also important to remember that change takes time and effort. Overcoming limiting beliefs is a process, and it's important to be patient and persistent. We may encounter setbacks along the way, but it's important to remember that these are just temporary and that with determination and perseverance, we can overcome any limiting belief and achieve our goals.

In conclusion, limiting beliefs can hold us back from reaching our full potential, but with the right tools and strategies, we can overcome them. By identifying our limiting beliefs, challenging them, replacing them with positive, empowering beliefs, practicing mindfulness, taking action, and being patient and persistent, we can break free from their hold and achieve greater success and fulfillment in our lives. Remember that change takes time and effort, but with determination and perseverance, anything is possible.

# 05: Mindset Mastery for Success

Mindset mastery is the key to achieving success in any area of life. It is the process of developing a positive and empowering mindset that allows you to overcome obstacles, set and achieve goals, and live a fulfilling life. In this chapter, we will explore the concept of mindset mastery and how you can use it to achieve success in your own life.

First, it is important to understand that mindset is the way that we think and perceive the world around us. Our mindset shapes our beliefs, attitudes, and behaviors, and ultimately determines our level of success in different areas of life. A positive and empowering mindset is essential for success, as it allows us to overcome obstacles, set and achieve goals, and live a fulfilling life.

One of the most important aspects of mindset mastery is the ability to control our thoughts. Our thoughts have a powerful impact on our emotions and behaviors, and we must learn to control them in order to achieve success. This means learning to identify and challenge negative thoughts, and replacing them with positive, empowering ones. It also means learning to focus on the present moment, rather than dwelling on the past or worrying about the future.

Another important aspect of mindset mastery is the ability to set and achieve goals. Setting and achieving goals is essential for success, as it allows us to move forward and make progress in our lives. However, it is important to set realistic and achievable goals, and to develop a plan for achieving them. This means breaking down larger goals into smaller, more manageable steps, and taking action towards achieving them on a regular basis.

In order to achieve success, it is also important to develop a growth mindset. A growth mindset is the belief that we can continue to grow and improve, regardless of our current circumstances. This means being open to new challenges, learning from our mistakes, and seeing failure as an opportunity to grow and learn. It also means being willing to take risks and try new things, even if there is a chance of failure.

In addition to developing a growth mindset, it is also important to develop a sense of self-awareness. Self-awareness is the ability to understand and accept our own strengths and weaknesses, and to use them to our advantage. This means taking the time to reflect on our own thoughts, emotions, and behaviors, and learning from them. It also means being honest with ourselves about our own limitations, and taking steps to overcome them.

Finally, it is important to develop a sense of resilience. Resilience is the ability to bounce back from setbacks and challenges, and to keep moving forward. This means learning to cope with difficult situations and to stay positive, even when things are not going well. It also means learning to take care of ourselves, both physically and mentally, in order to maintain our energy and motivation.

In conclusion, mindset mastery is the key to achieving success in any area of life. It is the process of developing a positive and empowering mindset that allows us to overcome obstacles, set and achieve goals, and live a fulfilling life. By learning to control our thoughts, set and achieve goals, develop a growth mindset, develop a sense of self-awareness, and develop a sense of resilience, we can master our mindsets and achieve success in all areas of our lives.

One practical way to apply the concepts of mindset mastery is through the use of affirmations. Affirmations are positive statements that we repeat to ourselves on a regular basis, in order to change our thoughts and beliefs. They can be used to challenge negative thoughts, reinforce positive beliefs, and set and achieve goals. For example, if you are struggling with self-doubt, you might use the affirmation "I am capable and worthy of success." If you are trying to overcome a fear, you might use the affirmation "I am courageous and strong." By repeating these affirmations on a regular basis, you can begin to change your thoughts and beliefs, and achieve a more positive and empowering mindset.

Another practical way to apply the concepts of mindset mastery is through visualization. Visualization is the process of creating a mental image of a desired outcome or goal. By visualizing the outcome that you want to achieve, you can create a more powerful and realistic image in your mind, which can help you to take the necessary steps to achieve that goal. For example, if you want to achieve a certain level of success in your career, you might visualize yourself in that role, and imagine the feelings and actions that would be necessary to achieve that level of success.

In addition, practicing mindfulness and meditation is a powerful tool for mastering your mindset. Mindfulness is the practice of being present and aware in the moment, without judgment. By practicing mindfulness, you can learn to be more aware of your thoughts and emotions, and to respond to them in a more constructive and positive way. Meditation is a powerful tool for reducing stress, increasing focus, and improving overall well-being. It can help you to develop a more positive and empowering mindset by increasing your awareness of your thoughts and emotions, and teaching you how to control them.

Finally, it is important to surround yourself with positive and supportive people. The people we surround ourselves with can have a powerful influence on our thoughts, emotions, and behaviors. By surrounding yourself with positive and supportive people, you can learn to think and act in a more positive and empowering way. This means seeking out the company of people who are positive, supportive, and encouraging, and limiting your exposure to people who are negative and critical.

In conclusion, mindset mastery is the key to achieving success in any area of life. By learning to control our thoughts, set and achieve goals, develop a growth mindset, develop a sense of self-awareness, and develop a sense of resilience, we can master our mindsets and achieve success in all areas of our lives. Practicing affirmations, visualization, mindfulness, meditation and surrounding yourself with positive people are powerful tools that can help us to achieve a positive and empowering mindset. Remember, success starts with a positive mindset, so take the time to master your mindset and enjoy the rewards of a successful life.

# 06: Personal Development for Growth

Personal development is the process of improving oneself in various areas of life, including emotional, physical, intellectual, and spiritual well-being. It involves setting goals, taking action, and making changes to improve one's overall quality of life. Personal development is an ongoing journey that requires commitment, self-awareness, and a willingness to learn and grow.

One of the key components of personal development is setting goals. Goals give direction and purpose to one's life, and provide a sense of accomplishment when achieved. It is important to set realistic and attainable goals that align with one's values and passions. It is also important to break down large goals into smaller, more manageable steps, and to track progress and celebrate successes along the way.

Another important aspect of personal development is self-awareness. This involves understanding one's thoughts, feelings, and behaviors, and how they affect one's life. Self-awareness allows individuals to identify areas where they need to improve and make necessary changes. It also enables them to be more mindful and present in the moment, and to make more conscious choices.

Personal development also requires taking action. This means being willing to step out of one's comfort zone, to try new things, and to take risks. It also means being open to learning and growth, and being willing to receive feedback and make necessary changes. It is important to remember that failure is a natural part of the learning process, and that it is through failure that we learn and grow.

In addition to the above, personal development also requires maintaining balance in one's life. This means taking care of one's physical and emotional well-being, and making time for self-care and relaxation. It also means maintaining healthy relationships, both with oneself and with others, and making time for leisure and hobbies.

Personal development is also about being of service to others. This means being kind and compassionate, and making a positive impact in the world. It also means being a role model and mentor to others, and sharing one's knowledge and experience to help others grow and develop.

In conclusion, personal development is a lifelong journey that requires commitment, self-awareness, and a willingness to learn and grow. It is about setting and achieving goals, taking action, maintaining balance, and being of service to others. It is a process that requires patience, perseverance, and a positive attitude, and it is through personal development that we can reach our full potential and live a fulfilling life.

Another important aspect of personal development is developing a growth mindset. A growth mindset is the belief that one's abilities and intelligence can be developed and improved through effort and learning. This mindset is in contrast to a fixed mindset, which is the belief that one's abilities and intelligence are set and cannot be changed.

Having a growth mindset is important for personal development because it allows individuals to embrace challenges and failures as opportunities for growth and learning. It also promotes resilience and perseverance in the face of adversity.

To develop a growth mindset, it is important to focus on the process of learning and growth, rather than the outcome. This means setting goals that are challenging but achievable, and being willing to put in the effort and work to achieve them. It also means being open to feedback, and using it as a tool for improvement.

Another way to develop a growth mindset is to surround oneself with people who have a growth mindset. This includes seeking out mentors and role models who embody the qualities of a growth mindset, and surrounding oneself with people who are supportive and encouraging of learning and growth.

In addition to all the above, personal development also involves developing emotional intelligence. Emotional intelligence is the ability to understand and manage one's own emotions, as well as the emotions of others. It is an important aspect of personal development because it allows individuals to communicate effectively, build and maintain relationships, and make better decisions.

To develop emotional intelligence, it is important to be aware of one's own emotions and how they affect one's thoughts and behaviors. It also means being able to identify and express emotions in a healthy way, and being able to empathize with and understand the emotions of others.

In conclusion, personal development is an ongoing journey

that requires commitment, self-awareness, and a willingness to learn and grow. It is about setting and achieving goals, taking action, maintaining balance, being of service to others, and developing a growth mindset and emotional intelligence. With the right mindset and approach, personal development can lead to a more fulfilling and satisfying life.

# 07: Building Resilience and Mental Toughness

Building resilience and mental toughness are essential skills for anyone looking to achieve success in life. These skills enable individuals to face challenges and adversity with determination, grit, and a positive attitude. In this chapter, we will explore the key concepts of resilience and mental toughness, as well as strategies for developing these skills.

Resilience is the ability to bounce back from difficult situations, to adapt to change, and to recover from setbacks. It is the capacity to maintain a positive outlook and to find meaning and purpose in adversity. Resilience is a key ingredient in mental toughness, which is the ability to perform at your best, even in the face of stress, pressure, and adversity.

There are several key strategies for building resilience and mental toughness. These include:

– Mindfulness: Mindfulness is the practice of being present in the moment and paying attention to your thoughts and emotions. It can help you to manage stress, improve focus, and build resilience.

## 07: BUILDING RESILIENCE AND MENTAL TOUGHNESS

– Positive Thinking: Focusing on positive thoughts and attitudes can help to build resilience and mental toughness. It is important to surround yourself with positive people and to think positively about yourself and your abilities.

– Exercise: Regular exercise has been shown to improve mood, reduce stress, and boost resilience. Engage in physical activities that you enjoy, such as running, cycling, or swimming.

– Sleep: Getting a good night's sleep is essential for maintaining good mental health and building resilience. Aim for 7-9 hours of sleep each night.

– Support Network: Building a strong support network of family and friends can help to provide emotional support and a sense of belonging. Surround yourself with people who will encourage and support you.

– Set goals: Setting goals gives you a sense of direction and purpose. It can help you to focus on what you want to achieve and to work towards it. Set both short-term and long-term goals and make a plan to achieve them.

– Learn from failure: Failure is a part of life, and it is important to learn from it. When things don't go as planned, use it as an opportunity to learn and grow. Failure can be a valuable teacher and can help you to build resilience and mental toughness.

– Practice Gratitude: Practicing gratitude can help to shift your focus from negative thoughts and emotions to positive ones. It can also help you to appreciate what you have and to develop a sense of contentment.

–Seek professional help: If you are struggling with mental health issues or are feeling overwhelmed, seek professional help. A therapist or counselor can help you to work through your feelings and to develop strategies for building resilience and mental toughness.

In conclusion, building resilience and mental toughness is essential for achieving success in life. It enables individuals to face challenges and adversity with determination, grit, and a positive attitude. By incorporating mindfulness, positive thinking, exercise, sleep, a support network, setting goals, learning from failure, practicing gratitude and seeking professional help, you can develop these skills and become more resilient and mentally tough.

Another important aspect of building resilience and mental toughness is learning to manage stress. Stress is a natural part of life, but when it becomes chronic, it can have a negative impact on our physical and mental health. Chronic stress can lead to conditions such as depression, anxiety, and heart disease.

One way to manage stress is through stress-reduction techniques such as deep breathing, progressive muscle relaxation, and meditation. These techniques can help to calm the mind and relax the body, making it easier to handle stress.

Another way to manage stress is through time management. Being able to effectively manage your time can help you to prioritize tasks, avoid procrastination, and reduce feelings of overwhelm. This can help to reduce stress and improve your overall well-being.

It is also important to maintain a healthy lifestyle. Eating a balanced diet, getting regular exercise, and getting enough sleep are all important for maintaining good physical and mental health. These activities can help to reduce stress and improve overall well-being.

Another important aspect of building resilience and mental

toughness is learning to develop a growth mindset. People with a growth mindset believe that their abilities can be developed through effort and learning. They view challenges and failures as opportunities for growth and learning. On the other hand, people with a fixed mindset believe that their abilities are fixed and cannot be changed. They tend to avoid challenges and give up easily when faced with difficulty.

Adopting a growth mindset can help you to become more resilient and mentally tough. It can help you to view challenges and setbacks as opportunities for growth and learning, rather than as personal failures. This can help you to develop a more positive attitude and to become more resilient in the face of adversity.

Finally, it is important to remember that building resilience and mental toughness takes time and effort. It is not something that can be achieved overnight. It is a lifelong process that requires patience, perseverance, and a willingness to learn and grow. With the right mindset and strategies, anyone can develop these important skills and become more resilient and mentally tough.

In conclusion, building resilience and mental toughness is a lifelong process that requires patience, perseverance and the right mindset. By incorporating mindfulness, positive thinking, exercise, sleep, a support network, setting goals, learning from failure, practicing gratitude, seeking professional help, managing stress, maintaining a healthy lifestyle, developing a growth mindset and time management, you can develop these skills and become more resilient and mentally tough. This will help you to face challenges and adversity with determination, grit, and a positive attitude, and to achieve your goals and aspirations in life.

# 08: Embracing Failure and Learning from Mistakes

Embracing failure and learning from mistakes is an essential part of personal and professional growth. The ability to recognize and learn from failure is a key component of success, as it enables individuals and organizations to identify and correct their weaknesses, leading to improved performance and increased effectiveness.

One of the most important things to understand about failure is that it is a natural and inevitable part of life. No one is immune to failure, and everyone makes mistakes. This is especially true when it comes to learning and trying new things. The key to success is not avoiding failure, but rather embracing it and using it as a learning opportunity.

When we fail, it is important to take a step back and assess what went wrong. This process of reflection and analysis can help us to identify the specific mistakes that were made, as well as the underlying causes of those mistakes. By understanding the root causes of our failures, we can take steps to prevent them from happening again in the future.

It is also important to remember that failure is not always a bad thing. In fact, many of the most successful people in history have failed multiple times before achieving success. Thomas Edison, for example, is said to have failed over 1000 times before finally inventing the light bulb. He famously said "I have not failed. I've just found 10,000 ways that won't work." Failure can be a source of valuable information and can help us to learn and grow in ways that success alone cannot.

Another key aspect of embracing failure and learning from mistakes is developing a growth mindset. A growth mindset is the belief that one's abilities and intelligence can be developed through effort and learning. This mindset is in contrast to a fixed mindset, which holds that one's abilities and intelligence are fixed and cannot be changed. Those with a growth mindset view failure as an opportunity to learn and grow, while those with a fixed mindset tend to view failure as a personal failure and give up easily.

In order to develop a growth mindset, it is important to focus on the process of learning and improvement, rather than the outcome. Instead of fixating on the end result, focus on the steps you are taking to achieve it. This will help you to stay motivated and resilient in the face of failure.

It is also important to develop a sense of self-compassion. Be kind to yourself when you make mistakes and remember that everyone fails. Don't beat yourself up over your failures and instead focus on the lessons you can learn from them.

In addition, it is important to surround yourself with supportive people who will encourage and support you in your efforts to learn from your mistakes. Having a supportive network can help you to stay motivated and on track, even when things get tough.

In conclusion, embracing failure and learning from mistakes is an essential part of personal and professional growth. Failure is a natural and inevitable part of life and should be viewed as an opportunity to learn and grow. By understanding the root causes of our failures, developing a growth mindset, and surrounding ourselves with supportive people, we can learn from our mistakes and achieve greater success in the long run.

Another important aspect of embracing failure and learning from mistakes is the ability to take action and make meaningful changes. Simply recognizing and analyzing your failures is not enough; you must also take concrete steps to address the issues that led to those failures. This could involve making changes to your habits, processes, or systems, or seeking out additional training or resources to help you improve.

One way to take action and make meaningful changes is to set specific, measurable goals for yourself. Setting clear, measurable goals will give you a sense of direction and purpose, and will help you to stay focused and motivated as you work to overcome your failures. Additionally, tracking your progress and measuring your results will help you to see the impact of your efforts and make any necessary adjustments.

Another important aspect is to be open to feedback and willing to listen to others. Feedback is a valuable tool for learning and growth, and it can help you to identify areas where you need to improve. Be open to constructive criticism and take it as an opportunity to learn and grow. Additionally, seek out feedback from a diverse group of people, including mentors, peers, and subordinates.

It's also important to learn to accept responsibility for your mistakes and not to blame others or external factors. Blaming others or external factors for your failures will only serve to hold you back from learning and growing. Instead, take ownership of your mistakes and use them as an opportunity to learn and improve.

Finally, it's essential to be patient with yourself. Changing habits and learning new skills takes time, and progress will not always be linear. Be patient with yourself and give yourself time to learn and grow. Remember that failure is a natural part of the learning process and it's not the end of the journey.

In summary, embracing failure and learning from mistakes is an essential part of personal and professional growth. It's important to understand that failure is a natural and inevitable part of life and to view it as an opportunity to learn and grow. Develop a growth mindset, surround yourself with supportive people, take action and make meaningful changes, be open to feedback, accept responsibility, and be patient with yourself. By doing these things, you will be able to learn from your mistakes and achieve greater success in the long run.

# 09: Time Management and Productivity

Time management and productivity are essential skills for achieving success in both personal and professional settings. By managing your time effectively, you can accomplish more in less time, reduce stress, and improve overall satisfaction with your life.

The first step in effective time management is setting clear goals. Without goals, it is difficult to know what to prioritize and how to allocate your time. Setting specific, measurable, achievable, relevant, and time-bound (SMART) goals can help you stay focused and motivated.

Next, it is important to create a schedule or to-do list. This can be done using a variety of tools such as a calendar, a planner, or a productivity app. Make sure to include all of your daily tasks, as well as any upcoming deadlines or appointments. Prioritize your tasks based on their importance and urgency.

One effective technique for managing your time is the Pomodoro Technique. This method involves breaking your work into 25-minute intervals, called "Pomodoros," with short breaks in between. After four Pomodoros, take a longer break to rest and recharge. This technique helps to increase focus and prevent burnout.

Another key aspect of time management is learning to say "no." Many people struggle with overcommitment, leading to feelings of overwhelm and stress. By being selective about what you take on, you can focus on the most important tasks and avoid unnecessary distractions.

Additionally, it is important to minimize interruptions and distractions. This can be done by turning off notifications on your phone, closing unnecessary tabs on your computer, and working in a quiet, distraction-free environment.

One of the most effective ways to boost productivity is to stay organized. Having a clean and organized workspace can help you stay focused and reduce stress. Additionally, taking the time to declutter and organize your digital life can help you be more productive.

Another way to boost productivity is to take regular breaks. Taking short breaks throughout the day can help improve focus and creativity, and prevent burnout.

Finally, it is important to practice self-care and maintain a healthy work-life balance. This can include things like getting enough sleep, eating well, and engaging in regular physical activity. Additionally, make sure to set aside time for leisure and relaxation to avoid burnout.

In conclusion, time management and productivity are essential skills for achieving success in both personal and professional settings. By setting clear goals, creating a schedule, using effective techniques, minimizing interruptions and distractions, staying organized, taking regular breaks, and practicing self-care, you can improve your productivity and achieve a better work-life balance.

Another key aspect of time management is delegation. Many people try to do everything themselves, leading to feelings of burnout and a lack of productivity. By delegating tasks to others, you can focus on the most important tasks and achieve more in less time.

When delegating tasks, it is important to choose the right person for the job. Consider the skills and experience of the person you are delegating to, and make sure they have the necessary resources and support to complete the task successfully.

It is also important to provide clear instructions and expectations when delegating tasks. This will help ensure that the task is completed correctly and on time.

Another way to boost productivity is through the use of technology. There are many productivity apps and tools available that can help you stay organized, manage your schedule, and track your progress.

One popular app is Trello, which allows you to create boards and cards for different tasks and projects. This can help you stay organized and on top of your to-do list.

Another app is RescueTime, which tracks your activity on your device and provides reports on how you spend your time. This can help you identify areas where you might be wasting time and make adjustments to your schedule.

Finally, it is important to remember that time management and productivity are ongoing processes. You will encounter obstacles and setbacks along the way, but by remaining focused and committed to your goals, you can continue to improve your productivity and achieve your desired results.

## 09: TIME MANAGEMENT AND PRODUCTIVITY

In conclusion, time management and productivity are essential skills that can help you achieve success in both personal and professional settings. By setting clear goals, creating a schedule, using effective techniques, minimizing interruptions and distractions, staying organized, taking regular breaks, practicing self-care, delegating tasks, and utilizing technology, you can improve your productivity and achieve a better work-life balance. Remember that time management and productivity are ongoing process and will require consistent effort and focus to maintain.

# 10: Building Strong Relationships

Building strong relationships is a key aspect of human life. Whether it is a romantic relationship, a friendship, or a professional partnership, having a network of supportive and trustworthy people is essential for our well-being and happiness. However, building strong relationships can be challenging, as it requires effort, communication, and a willingness to be vulnerable. In this chapter, we will explore some of the key elements of building strong relationships and discuss strategies for maintaining and strengthening them.

One of the most important elements of building strong relationships is effective communication. Communication is the foundation upon which all relationships are built, and it is essential for understanding and connecting with others. When communicating with others, it is important to be clear and direct, to listen actively, and to express ourselves honestly and authentically. Additionally, it is essential to be aware of nonverbal cues and to pay attention to how our words and actions are being received.

Another key element of building strong relationships is trust. Trust is the foundation of any healthy relationship and is built over time through consistency, honesty, and reliability. Trust is also built through vulnerability, which allows us to open up and share our thoughts, feelings, and experiences with others. When we are vulnerable, we are able to build deeper connections with others and create a sense of intimacy.

Empathy is also crucial for building strong relationships. Empathy is the ability to understand and share the feelings of others, and it is essential for building trust and understanding. When we are able to put ourselves in the shoes of others and understand their perspective, we are better able to communicate and connect with them. Additionally, empathy helps us to be more compassionate and understanding, which can lead to deeper and more meaningful relationships.

Another key element of building strong relationships is shared values and goals. When we share similar values and goals with others, we are more likely to connect with them and form a deeper bond. Additionally, shared values and goals provide a sense of purpose and direction, which can help to strengthen relationships over time.

Finally, building strong relationships also requires a willingness to compromise and to work through conflicts. Conflict is a natural part of any relationship, and it is essential to learn how to handle it in a healthy and constructive way. This requires effective communication, empathy, and a willingness to see things from the other person's perspective. Additionally, it is important to be willing to compromise and to work together to find a solution that is acceptable to both parties.

In conclusion, building strong relationships is an essential aspect of human life and requires effort, communication, and a willingness to be vulnerable. To build strong relationships, it is important to communicate effectively, build trust, practice empathy, share values and goals, and be willing to compromise and work through conflicts. By implementing these strategies, we can create deep and meaningful connections with others and improve our overall well-being and happiness.

Another important aspect of building strong relationships is being reliable and dependable. When we make commitments, it is important to follow through on them and to be there for the people we care about. Being dependable builds trust and shows that we are committed to the relationship.

It's also important to be flexible and open to change. Relationships can change over time, and it's important to be willing to adapt and evolve as needed. This can include learning new things about each other, trying new activities, or even changing the nature of the relationship. Being open to change allows us to grow together and deepen our connection.

Additionally, it is important to show appreciation and gratitude towards the people in our lives. Expressing gratitude and appreciation helps to build positive feelings and can strengthen the bond in a relationship. A simple thank you or a thoughtful gesture can go a long way in showing someone that we appreciate them.

It's also important to set boundaries and respect the boundaries of others. In any relationship, it's important to have a clear understanding of what is and isn't acceptable behavior. Setting boundaries allows us to maintain our sense of self and ensures that we are treated with respect. Additionally, when we respect the boundaries of others, we are showing them that we care about their well-being and are committed to the relationship.

In addition to all the above, it is also important to always be open to learning and growing. This means being open to feedback, taking the time to reflect on our actions and behavior, and being willing to make changes when necessary. Additionally, it means being open to learning about others and their perspectives, which can help us to build deeper connections and understanding.

Finally, building strong relationships also require patience and consistency. As with anything worthwhile, building and maintaining strong relationships takes time and effort. It requires patience to work through challenges and consistency in our actions and behavior. It's important to remember that relationships are not always easy, but with patience and consistency, they can be incredibly rewarding.

In conclusion, building strong relationships is a complex and multi-faceted process that requires effort, communication, trust, empathy, shared values, goals and the willingness to work through conflicts, be reliable and dependable, be flexible and open to change, show appreciation and gratitude, set boundaries and respect the boundaries of others, be open to learning and growing, and patience and consistency. By understanding and implementing these strategies, we can create deep, meaningful and long-lasting relationships that will enrich our lives and bring us happiness and fulfillment.

# 11: The Importance of Self-Care

Self-care is the practice of taking care of one's own physical, mental, and emotional well-being. It is an essential part of maintaining good health and overall well-being, and it is something that should be prioritized by everyone.

One of the main reasons why self-care is so important is that it helps us to manage stress. Stress is a normal part of life, but it can become overwhelming if it is not managed properly. When we practice self-care, we are taking steps to reduce stress and improve our overall well-being. This can include things like exercise, relaxation techniques, and healthy eating.

Another important aspect of self-care is that it helps us to be more present in our lives. When we are constantly busy and stressed, it can be difficult to focus on the present moment and enjoy the things that are happening around us. By taking care of ourselves, we can be more present and enjoy life more fully.

Self-care also helps us to be more resilient. When we are feeling stressed and overwhelmed, it can be difficult to bounce back from setbacks and challenges. By taking care of ourselves, we are building our resilience and our ability to cope with difficult situations.

One of the most important things to remember about self-care is that it is not a one-time thing. It is a ongoing process that requires consistent effort and attention. This can include setting aside time each day for self-care activities, such as exercise or meditation, as well as making sure to get enough sleep and eat a healthy diet.

It is also important to remember that self-care is not selfish. Taking care of ourselves is not only important for our own well-being, but it also allows us to be better equipped to help and support others.

One way to practice self-care is by setting boundaries. This means learning to say no to things that don't serve us, and prioritizing our own needs. This can be difficult for some people, as they may feel guilty or selfish for putting themselves first. However, setting boundaries is a vital part of self-care and can help us to avoid burnout and maintain a healthy balance in our lives.

Another way to practice self-care is by practicing mindfulness. This means being present in the moment and paying attention to our thoughts and feelings. This can help us to identify and address any negative thoughts or emotions that may be impacting our well-being.

Other self-care practices include exercise, journaling, reading, getting enough sleep, spending time in nature and socializing with loved ones.

In conclusion, self-care is an essential part of maintaining good health and overall well-being. It helps us to manage stress, be more present in our lives, be more resilient, and set boundaries. It is an ongoing process that requires consistent effort and attention. By making self-care a priority, we can improve our overall well-being and enjoy life more fully.

Another important aspect of self-care is self-compassion. Self-compassion involves treating ourselves with kindness and understanding, rather than judgment and criticism. It involves recognizing that we all have flaws and make mistakes, and that this is a normal part of being human.

When we practice self-compassion, we are more likely to be resilient in the face of challenges, and less likely to be overwhelmed by negative emotions. We are also more likely to set realistic goals for ourselves, and to treat ourselves kindly when we fall short of these goals.

Self-compassion can be practiced in a variety of ways. One way is through self-compassionate self-talk, which involves speaking to ourselves in a kind and understanding way. This can involve reframing negative thoughts and emotions, and reminding ourselves that we are not alone in our struggles.

Another way to practice self-compassion is through mindfulness. This means being present in the moment and paying attention to our thoughts and feelings without judgment. Mindfulness can help us to be more compassionate towards ourselves, as we learn to accept ourselves as we are, rather than constantly striving for perfection.

Self-compassion can also be practiced through self-care activities such as exercise, journaling, and spending time in nature. These activities can help us to feel more relaxed and centered, which can in turn help us to be more compassionate towards ourselves.

In addition to self-compassion, self-care also includes self-awareness and self-exploration. This means taking the time to understand our own thoughts, feelings, and behaviors, and to explore what is truly important to us. By gaining a deeper understanding of ourselves, we can make more informed decisions about how to take care of ourselves and live a fulfilling life.

Self-care is also important for our relationships. When we take care of ourselves, we are better equipped to be there for others and to build healthy and meaningful relationships. When we neglect our own well-being, we may find ourselves feeling resentful and disconnected from others.

In conclusion, self-care is a vital component of overall well-being and is essential for managing stress, being present, being resilient, setting boundaries, practicing self-compassion and self-awareness, and fostering healthy relationships. It is not a luxury, but a necessity. It is important to make self-care a priority, and to find ways to incorporate it into our daily lives. By doing so, we can enjoy a more fulfilling and meaningful life.

# 12: Unlocking Your Creativity and Innovation

Unlocking Your Creativity and Innovation

Creativity and innovation are essential for personal and professional growth, as well as for the advancement of society. They are the driving forces behind new ideas, products, and solutions. However, many people feel that they are not creative or innovative and struggle to generate new ideas. The good news is that creativity and innovation are skills that can be developed and nurtured. In this chapter, we will explore ways to unlock your creativity and innovation and bring new ideas to life.

First, it is important to understand that creativity and innovation are not the same thing. Creativity refers to the ability to generate new ideas, while innovation refers to the ability to put those ideas into action. Creativity is the spark, and innovation is the fire. Both are important for creating new and valuable things.

One key to unlocking your creativity is to be open to new experiences and perspectives. This means exposing yourself to diverse people, cultures, and ideas. It also means being willing to take risks and try new things, even if they seem strange or uncomfortable at first. This kind of open-mindedness can help you see the world in new ways and generate new ideas.

Another key to unlocking your creativity is to be curious. Curiosity is the desire to learn and understand more about the world around you. It is the drive to ask questions and seek answers. Being curious means being open to new information and being willing to explore new areas of knowledge. This kind of curiosity can help you see connections and patterns that others might miss, which can lead to new ideas.

Another way to unlock your creativity and innovation is to be willing to play and experiment. Play is a powerful tool for generating new ideas. It allows you to relax, let go of your preconceptions, and explore new possibilities. Experimenting allows you to test different ideas and see what works and what doesn't. This kind of experimentation and play can help you find new solutions to problems and create new products.

Another way to boost creativity and innovation is to collaborate with others. Collaboration allows you to share ideas and perspectives, which can lead to new and better ideas. It also allows you to combine different skills and talents to create something new. Collaboration can also increase accountability and motivation, which can help you stay focused and committed to your ideas.

To unleash your innovation, you need to be willing to take action. Innovation is not just about having good ideas, but also about putting those ideas into action. This means taking risks, making mistakes, and learning from them. It also means being willing to fail. Failure is a natural part of the innovation process and can provide valuable lessons and insights.

In addition to these general tips, there are specific techniques that can help you boost your creativity and innovation. One such technique is brainstorming. Brainstorming is a process of generating new ideas by free-associating and building on the ideas of others. To brainstorm effectively, it is important to set aside judgment, encourage wild ideas, and build on the ideas of others.

Another technique is lateral thinking. Lateral thinking is a process of solving problems by looking at them from different perspectives. This can involve looking at a problem from a different angle, using a different frame of reference, or using a different set of assumptions. Lateral thinking can help you generate new ideas and find new solutions to problems.

Finally, it is important to note that unlocking your creativity and innovation is not a one-time event but a continuous process. It requires regular practice, experimentation, and reflection. It also requires a willingness to change and adapt. By being open-minded, curious, playful, collaborative, and willing to take action, you can unlock your creativity and innovation and bring new ideas to life.

One way to continue the process of unlocking your creativity and innovation is to set aside dedicated time for brainstorming and idea generation. This can be done individually or as part of a group. It is also important to make space for experimentation and play in your daily routine. This can be done by setting aside time for hobbies or taking on new projects outside of your usual work.

Another way to continue the process is to seek feedback and input from others. This can be done by sharing your ideas with trusted colleagues or friends and asking for their thoughts and suggestions. It is also important to be open to constructive criticism and use it as a learning opportunity.

Finally, it is important to stay informed about the latest trends and developments in your field. This can be done by reading industry publications, attending conferences, and networking with other professionals. By staying up-to-date, you can gain new perspectives and insights that can lead to new ideas.

In conclusion, creativity and innovation are essential skills that can be developed and nurtured. By being open-minded, curious, playful, collaborative, and willing to take action, you can unlock your creativity and innovation and bring new ideas to life. It is important to set aside dedicated time for brainstorming and idea generation, seek feedback and input from others, and stay informed about the latest trends and developments in your field. By continuously working on your creativity and innovation, you can create new and valuable things, both for yourself and for the world.

# 13: Overcoming Fear and Anxiety

Fear and anxiety are natural human emotions that everyone experiences at some point in their lives. They are a response to perceived threats and can be helpful in certain situations, such as preparing for a job interview or keeping us safe from danger. However, when fear and anxiety become overwhelming and start to interfere with our daily lives, they can become a problem. This chapter will explore the causes of fear and anxiety, the differences between the two, and strategies for overcoming them.

Causes of Fear and Anxiety

Fear and anxiety are triggered by different situations and can be caused by a variety of factors. Some common causes include:

– Trauma or past experiences: Trauma, such as physical or emotional abuse, can cause long-term fear and anxiety.

– Genetics: Some people may be more prone to anxiety due to genetic factors.

– Brain chemistry: Imbalances in brain chemicals, such as serotonin and dopamine, can contribute to anxiety.

– Medical conditions: Certain medical conditions, such as heart disease or thyroid problems, can cause anxiety.

– Environmental factors: Stressful life events, such as a job loss or a move to a new place, can trigger fear and anxiety.

Differences between Fear and Anxiety

While fear and anxiety are closely related, they are not the same thing. Fear is a natural response to a specific, immediate threat. For example, if you see a snake in your path while hiking, you will feel fear. It's a natural response that prepares you to either fight or flee. Anxiety, on the other hand, is a general feeling of unease that can be caused by a wide range of things. It's a response to potential future threats, such as worrying about a job interview or a medical test.

Overcoming Fear and Anxiety

There are several strategies that can help you overcome fear and anxiety. These include:

– Cognitive-behavioral therapy (CBT): This type of therapy focuses on identifying and changing negative thoughts and behaviors that contribute to fear and anxiety.

– Exposure therapy: This type of therapy involves gradually exposing yourself to the thing that you fear in a controlled environment. This can help you learn that the feared thing is not as dangerous as you thought.

– Medication: Antidepressant and anti-anxiety medications can be effective in reducing fear and anxiety.

– Relaxation techniques: Relaxation techniques, such as deep breathing, yoga, and meditation, can help reduce stress and anxiety.

– Self-care: Taking care of yourself by getting enough sleep, eating well, and engaging in physical activity can help reduce anxiety and promote overall well-being.

Conclusion

Fear and anxiety are natural human emotions that can become a problem when they become overwhelming. Understanding the causes and differences between the two can help you develop strategies for overcoming them. Some effective strategies include cognitive-behavioral therapy, exposure therapy, medication, relaxation techniques and self-care. Remember, it is important to seek professional help if your fear or anxiety is interfering with your daily life. With the right strategies and support, it is possible to overcome fear and anxiety and lead a fulfilling life.

It's also important to note that overcoming fear and anxiety is not a one-time process, but rather a continuous journey. It's important to be patient with yourself and to not expect to be completely free from fear and anxiety overnight. Additionally, it's important to acknowledge that setbacks can happen, and that's okay. The important thing is to keep moving forward and to not let setbacks discourage you from continuing to work on overcoming your fears and anxieties.

Another strategy that can be helpful in overcoming fear and anxiety is mindfulness. Mindfulness is the practice of being present and fully engaged in the current moment, without judgment. Mindfulness can help reduce anxiety by helping you focus on the present rather than dwelling on the past or worrying about the future. Mindfulness practices such as meditation, yoga, or tai chi can help you develop mindfulness skills.

Another effective strategy is to practice self-compassion. Self-compassion involves treating yourself with the same kindness and understanding that you would offer to a friend. It also includes acknowledging that everyone makes mistakes and has difficult times, and that it's normal to struggle. When you're feeling anxious, try to remind yourself that it's normal to feel this way and that you're not alone.

Lastly, it's important to build a support system. Support from friends and family can be a powerful tool in overcoming fear and anxiety. Talking to someone you trust about your fears and anxieties can help you gain a different perspective and feel less alone. Joining a support group can also be helpful as it allows you to connect with others who are going through similar experiences.

In conclusion, fear and anxiety are natural human emotions that can become overwhelming. However, with the right strategies, support and patience, it's possible to overcome them and lead a fulfilling life. Remember to take it one step at a time, be patient with yourself and to seek professional help if needed.

# 14: Building Confidence and Self-Esteem

Building confidence and self-esteem is a vital aspect of personal development and can greatly impact an individual's ability to navigate through life's challenges. Confidence is the belief in one's own abilities, qualities, and judgments, while self-esteem is the overall sense of self-worth and value. Both are closely related and often work together to affect an individual's overall well-being.

There are several key strategies that can be used to build confidence and self-esteem. One of the most important is to set and achieve goals. Setting small, manageable goals for oneself can help to build confidence as one becomes more successful in achieving them. It is also important to have a positive attitude and to focus on the present moment, rather than dwelling on past failures or worrying about future challenges.

Another important strategy is to practice self-care and to engage in activities that promote physical and emotional well-being. This can include regular exercise, eating a healthy diet, getting enough sleep, and taking time to relax and de-stress. Additionally, surrounding oneself with positive and supportive people can also help to build confidence and self-esteem.

It's also important to practice self-compassion and self-acceptance, which means treating oneself with kindness and understanding, rather than harshly judging oneself for mistakes or perceived shortcomings. This means being kind and forgiving towards oneself, and to take a more positive and understanding perspective of oneself.

Another effective way to build confidence and self-esteem is to challenge negative thoughts and beliefs. Negative thoughts and beliefs can be limiting, and can prevent an individual from reaching their full potential. By recognizing and challenging negative thoughts, one can begin to replace them with more positive and empowering thoughts.

It's also important to be mindful of one's self-talk and to be aware of the language and phrases we use to describe ourselves and our abilities. Instead of using negative or self-deprecating language, it's important to use positive and empowering language to describe oneself.

Lastly, it's important to remember that building confidence and self-esteem is a continuous process that takes time and effort. It's important to be patient and compassionate with oneself and to remember that setbacks and failures are a normal part of the process. It's also important to remember that there is no "perfect" level of confidence or self-esteem and that everyone's journey is unique.

In conclusion, building confidence and self-esteem is an important aspect of personal development that can greatly impact an individual's ability to navigate through life's challenges. By setting and achieving goals, practicing self-care, surrounding oneself with positive and supportive people, practicing self-compassion and self-acceptance, challenging negative thoughts and beliefs, being mindful of one's self-talk, and being patient and compassionate with oneself, one can begin to build and maintain confidence and self-esteem. Remember, it's a continuous journey and it's important to be kind and compassionate with oneself through the process.

Another important aspect of building confidence and self-esteem is learning to embrace and accept one's uniqueness. Everyone is different and has their own unique set of strengths, weaknesses, and experiences. It is important to focus on and appreciate one's own individuality, rather than constantly comparing oneself to others or trying to conform to societal norms. Embracing one's uniqueness can help to build self-acceptance and self-confidence.

Another important tool for building confidence and self-esteem is positive affirmations. Positive affirmations are statements that are repeated to oneself with the intention of promoting a positive mindset and attitude. Examples of positive affirmations include "I am worthy", "I am capable", "I am strong", "I am in control of my thoughts and emotions". Repeating these affirmations to oneself on a daily basis can help to change negative thought patterns and promote a more positive and confident mindset.

It is also important to learn how to handle criticism and constructive feedback in a healthy way. Criticism and feedback can be difficult to hear, but they can also be valuable tools for growth and improvement. Instead of taking criticism and feedback personally, it is important to approach them objectively and use them as opportunities to learn and improve.

In addition to these strategies, it can also be helpful to seek professional support such as therapy or counseling. A therapist or counselor can help to identify and work through underlying issues that may be contributing to low confidence and self-esteem. They can also provide additional strategies and tools for building confidence and self-esteem.

Lastly, it's important to remember that building confidence and self-esteem is a continuous process that takes time and effort. It's important to be patient and compassionate with oneself and to remember that setbacks and failures are a normal part of the process. It's also important to remember that there is no "perfect" level of confidence or self-esteem and that everyone's journey is unique.

In conclusion, building confidence and self-esteem is an important aspect of personal development that can greatly impact an individual's ability to navigate through life's challenges. By setting and achieving goals, practicing self-care, surrounding oneself with positive and supportive people, practicing self-compassion and self-acceptance, challenging negative thoughts and beliefs, being mindful of one's self-talk, and being patient and compassionate with oneself, embracing one's uniqueness, using positive affirmations, handling criticism and feedback in a healthy way, and seeking professional support can all be effective ways to build and maintain confidence and self-esteem. Remember, it's a continuous journey and it's important to be kind and compassionate with oneself through the process.

# 15: Harnessing the Power of Positive Thinking

The power of positive thinking is a powerful tool that can help individuals achieve their goals and lead happier, more fulfilling lives. Positive thinking is the practice of focusing on the good in any situation and maintaining a positive outlook, even in the face of adversity. By harnessing the power of positive thinking, individuals can overcome challenges, improve their mental and physical health, and achieve greater success in their personal and professional lives.

One of the key benefits of positive thinking is that it can help individuals to overcome obstacles and achieve their goals. When faced with a difficult task or challenge, those who maintain a positive outlook are more likely to find solutions and persist in the face of adversity. This is because positive thinking allows individuals to see the best in any situation, even when things are not going well. By focusing on the good, individuals can find the motivation and inspiration they need to continue working towards their goals, even when things get tough.

Another important benefit of positive thinking is that it can improve mental and physical health. Positive thinking is associated with lower levels of stress and anxiety, and has been shown to boost the immune system, decrease the risk of heart disease, and reduce symptoms of depression and other mental health conditions. This is because positive thinking helps individuals to focus on the present moment and find the good in any situation, rather than dwelling on the past or worrying about the future.

In addition to these benefits, positive thinking can also lead to greater success in both personal and professional life. Positive thinking can help individuals to build stronger relationships, become more successful in their careers, and achieve greater financial success. This is because individuals who maintain a positive outlook are more likely to be confident, optimistic, and motivated, which are all traits that are highly valued by employers and others in the professional world.

One of the most effective ways to harness the power of positive thinking is to practice daily affirmations. Affirmations are positive statements that individuals can repeat to themselves on a regular basis to help them focus on the good in any situation. For example, an affirmation might be "I am strong and capable of achieving my goals" or "I am surrounded by love and support." By repeating these affirmations on a daily basis, individuals can train their minds to focus on the positive, which can help them to overcome challenges and achieve greater success.

Another effective way to harness the power of positive thinking is to practice gratitude. Gratitude is the practice of focusing on the things in one's life that one is thankful for, rather than dwelling on the things that are missing. By taking time each day to reflect on the things that one is grateful for, individuals can shift their focus from negative thoughts to positive ones, which can help them to maintain a more positive outlook.

Finally, it is important to surround oneself with positive people. Surrounding oneself with positive people can help to create a supportive environment that encourages positive thinking. Being around positive people can help to reduce stress, improve mental and physical health, and provide support and encouragement when things get tough.

In conclusion, the power of positive thinking is a powerful tool that can help individuals to achieve their goals, improve their mental and physical health, and lead happier, more fulfilling lives. By harnessing the power of positive thinking through techniques such as affirmations, gratitude, and surrounding oneself with positive people, individuals can overcome challenges and achieve greater success in their personal and professional lives.

Another important aspect of harnessing the power of positive thinking is to develop a growth mindset. A growth mindset is the belief that one's abilities and intelligence can be developed and improved through effort and learning. Individuals with a growth mindset are more likely to take on challenges, persist in the face of failure, and see setbacks as opportunities for growth and learning.

One way to develop a growth mindset is to challenge negative thoughts and beliefs. When faced with a negative thought or belief, such as "I can't do this" or "I'm not good enough," individuals can challenge these thoughts by asking themselves questions such as "What evidence do I have for this thought?" and "Is there a different way to think about this situation?" By questioning negative thoughts and beliefs, individuals can begin to shift their perspective and develop a more positive and growth-oriented mindset.

## 15: HARNESSING THE POWER OF POSITIVE THINKING

Another way to develop a growth mindset is to focus on progress rather than perfection. Perfectionism can lead to procrastination and a fear of failure, which can prevent individuals from taking action and achieving their goals. By focusing on progress rather than perfection, individuals can set realistic and attainable goals, take small steps towards achieving them, and see progress in their efforts.

It's also important to practice self-compassion. Self-compassion is the practice of being kind and understanding towards oneself, rather than being overly critical or self-judgmental. When individuals are self-compassionate, they are more likely to be resilient in the face of failure and setbacks, and are more likely to bounce back from difficult situations.

Finally, it's important to take care of one's physical and emotional well-being. Positive thinking and a positive attitude can help to improve one's overall well-being, but it's also important to take care of one's physical and emotional health. This includes getting enough sleep, eating a healthy diet, exercise, and engaging in activities that bring joy and relaxation.

In conclusion, harnessing the power of positive thinking is a powerful tool that can help individuals to achieve their goals, improve their mental and physical health, and lead happier, more fulfilling lives. By developing a growth mind-set, challenging negative thoughts, focusing on progress, practicing self-compassion, and taking care of one's physical and emotional well-being, individuals can achieve greater success in their personal and professional lives. By incorporating positive thinking into one's daily routine and making it a habit, individuals can reap the benefits of positive thinking in their life.

# 16: Financial Empowerment

Financial empowerment is the process of gaining control over one's finances, including understanding and managing one's income, expenses, and investments. It is a crucial aspect of overall well-being and can have a significant impact on an individual's quality of life. In this chapter, we will explore the various elements of financial empowerment and discuss strategies for achieving it.

One of the first steps in achieving financial empowerment is understanding one's current financial situation. This includes analyzing one's income, expenses, and debts. It is important to have a clear understanding of where one's money is coming from and where it is going in order to develop a budget and create a plan for achieving financial goals. A budget is a financial plan that outlines how much money is expected to be earned and spent in a given period of time. It is a useful tool for managing finances and can help individuals stay on track with their financial goals.

Another key aspect of financial empowerment is understanding and managing debt. Debt can take many forms, including credit card debt, student loans, and mortgages. It is important to understand the terms and conditions of any debt, as well as the interest rates and fees associated with it. By understanding and managing debt, individuals can reduce the amount of money they owe and increase their overall financial stability.

Investing is another important aspect of financial empowerment. Investing allows individuals to grow their wealth and create financial security for the future. There are many different types of investments, including stocks, bonds, and real estate. It is important to understand the different types of investments and the risks and potential returns associated with them. A financial advisor can help individuals make informed investment decisions and create a diversified portfolio that aligns with their goals and risk tolerance.

Another important aspect of financial empowerment is having access to financial education and resources. Financial education can help individuals understand how to manage their money, invest, and plan for the future. There are many resources available, including books, online courses, and workshops. It is also important to be aware of financial scams and fraud, and to seek help if needed.

Finally, it is important to have a plan for achieving financial goals. This includes setting realistic and achievable goals, such as saving for a down payment on a house or retirement. A plan also includes setting a timeline for achieving these goals, and tracking progress along the way.

In conclusion, financial empowerment is an ongoing process that requires knowledge, understanding, and management of one's finances. By understanding one's current financial situation, managing debt, investing, and having access to financial education and resources, individuals can gain control over their finances and create financial stability and security for themselves and their families.

One important aspect of financial empowerment is having an emergency fund. An emergency fund is a savings account that is set aside for unexpected expenses such as medical bills, car repairs, or job loss. Having an emergency fund can provide a safety net and help individuals avoid going into debt in case of unexpected events. It is recommended to have at least three to six months' worth of living expenses saved in an emergency fund.

Another way to achieve financial empowerment is by automating your savings. It's easy to put off saving for the future, but by setting up automatic transfers from your checking account to your savings account, you can ensure that a portion of your income is set aside for future goals. This can be done on a weekly or monthly basis, depending on your preference.

Another important aspect of financial empowerment is learning how to negotiate. Whether it's negotiating a raise at work or haggling with a salesperson, the ability to negotiate can help individuals save money and increase their income. Learning how to effectively communicate your value and negotiate can pay off in the long run.

In order to achieve financial empowerment, it is also important to have a clear understanding of your credit score. Your credit score is a three-digit number that lenders use to determine your creditworthiness. It is based on factors such as your payment history, outstanding debt, and length of credit history. A good credit score can help you qualify for lower interest rates on loans, credit cards, and mortgages, which can save you thousands of dollars over time.

Finally, it is important to have a long-term perspective on your finances. This means thinking about the future and planning for it. This includes planning for retirement, saving for your children's education, and creating a will. It also means thinking about the impact of your financial decisions on future generations. By taking a long-term perspective on your finances, you can make better decisions today that will benefit you and your family in the future.

In conclusion, financial empowerment is a multifaceted process that involves understanding and managing one's finances, setting and achieving financial goals, and having access to financial education and resources. By taking control of your finances and making informed decisions, you can create financial stability and security for yourself and your family.

# 17: Empowering Your Career

Empowering Your Career

Your career is one of the most important aspects of your life. It not only provides you with financial stability and security, but it also gives you a sense of purpose and fulfillment. However, many people feel stuck in their careers and struggle to take control of their professional development. In this chapter, we will explore ways to empower your career and take charge of your professional journey.

The first step to empowering your career is to set clear and specific goals. Without a clear destination in mind, it can be difficult to know what steps to take to achieve success. Start by identifying your long-term career aspirations and then break them down into smaller, more manageable goals. For example, if your ultimate goal is to become a manager, your short-term goals may include taking on additional responsibilities, developing new skills, and networking with other professionals in your field.

Once you have set your goals, it is important to create a plan to achieve them. This may involve taking on new responsibilities, seeking out new opportunities, or developing new skills. It is also important to stay organized and track your progress. This will help you stay motivated and on track, and it will also help you identify any obstacles that may be preventing you from achieving your goals.

Another key aspect of empowering your career is networking. The connections you make with other professionals in your field can be incredibly valuable. They can provide you with opportunities for advancement, mentorship, and support. To build a strong professional network, you should attend industry events, join professional organizations, and connect with other professionals on LinkedIn.

In addition to networking, it is also important to invest in your own professional development. This may involve taking classes, attending workshops, or pursuing additional certifications. By continually learning and growing, you will be better equipped to take on new challenges and advance in your career.

Another important aspect of empowering your career is to be proactive and take initiative. This means not waiting for opportunities to come to you, but rather seeking them out and creating them yourself. This could mean pitching new ideas to your manager, starting a side hustle, or seeking out a mentor. By being proactive, you will be more likely to achieve your goals and take control of your career.

Another important aspect of empowering your career is to continuously improve your communication skills. Whether it is verbal or written, communication is key in building professional relationships and in making progress in any field. Being able to communicate effectively will enable you to clearly articulate your ideas, negotiate effectively, and build stronger relationships with your colleagues and superiors.

Finally, it is important to have a positive attitude and to maintain a sense of perspective. Having a positive attitude will help you stay motivated and focused on your goals, even when faced with obstacles. Additionally, it is important to remember that success is a journey, not a destination. Empowering your career is not about achieving a single goal or reaching a certain level of success, but about continuously working towards your goals and growing as a professional.

In conclusion, empowering your career is about taking charge of your professional development and actively working towards your goals. This involves setting clear and specific goals, creating a plan to achieve them, networking, investing in your own professional development, being proactive, continuously improving your communication skills and maintaining a positive attitude. Remember, success is a journey, not a destination, and by continually working towards your goals and growing as a professional, you will be able to empower your career and take control of your professional journey.

Another important aspect of empowering your career is to understand and leverage your strengths. Everyone has unique strengths and abilities that can be used to excel in their chosen field. By understanding and utilizing your strengths, you can find a career path that is fulfilling and that allows you to make the most impact.

To understand your strengths, you can take a strengths assessment or simply reflect on what you enjoy doing and what you are naturally good at. Once you have a clear understanding of your strengths, you can start to look for opportunities that align with them. This could mean pursuing a specific role within your current company or looking for a new job that utilizes your strengths.

Along with understanding and leveraging your strengths, it's also important to be adaptable and open to change. The job market and the economy are constantly changing, and it's important to be able to adapt to these changes in order to stay competitive. This means being open to new technologies, new ways of working, and new business models. By being adaptable, you will be more likely to find opportunities and be successful in your career.

Another important aspect of empowering your career is to build a personal brand. Your personal brand is the image or reputation that you have in the professional world. It's how others see you and what they think of when they think of you. Building a strong personal brand can help you stand out in your field, increase your visibility, and open up new opportunities.

To build a strong personal brand, you should focus on consistently delivering high-quality work, building relationships, and being a thought leader in your field. This can be done by writing articles, giving presentations, and speaking at industry events. Additionally, you should use social media and professional networks to promote your work, connect with others in your field, and share your thoughts and insights.

Finally, it is important to have a work-life balance. Having a balance between your professional and personal life is crucial for your well-being and overall satisfaction with your career. A work-life balance allows you to have enough time for your family, friends and hobbies, and also helps to reduce stress and burnout.

In conclusion, empowering your career is about taking charge of your professional development and actively working towards your goals. This involves setting clear and specific goals, creating a plan to achieve them, networking, investing in your own professional development, being proactive, continuously improving your communication skills, maintaining a positive attitude, understanding and leveraging your strengths, being adaptable and open to change, building a personal brand and having a work-life balance. Remember, career empowerment is a continuous process, and by consistently working on these areas, you will be able to take control of your professional journey and achieve the success you desire.

# 18: Conclusion: Living an Empowered Life

Living an empowered life is about taking control of your own destiny and making the most out of your experiences. It is about recognizing that you have the power to shape your own reality and that you have the ability to create the life you want for yourself.

Empowerment starts with self-awareness. To live an empowered life, you must first understand who you are, what you stand for, and what you want out of life. This requires taking a step back and looking at yourself objectively, without judgment or preconceived notions. It means being honest with yourself about your strengths and weaknesses, and understanding what drives you.

Once you have a clear understanding of yourself, you can begin to set goals and create a vision for your future. Setting goals is an important step in the empowerment process, as it gives you something to work towards and provides a sense of direction and purpose. These goals should be specific, measurable, and achievable, and should align with your values and what you want to achieve in life.

# 18: CONCLUSION: LIVING AN EMPOWERED LIFE

The next step in living an empowered life is to take action. This means putting in the work to achieve your goals and making things happen. It means taking risks and being willing to fail, as failure is an important part of the learning and growth process. It also means being proactive and taking responsibility for your actions, rather than waiting for things to happen to you.

Another important aspect of living an empowered life is developing a positive mindset. This means learning to see the good in every situation, and understanding that every challenge is an opportunity to grow and learn. It also means being resilient in the face of adversity, and having the ability to bounce back from setbacks and failures.

In addition to personal development, living an empowered life also means being a positive influence on those around you. This means being a role model for others, and inspiring them to live their best lives. It means being a leader and making a difference in the world.

Ultimately, living an empowered life is about being true to yourself and living in alignment with your values and what is most important to you. It is about taking control of your own life and creating the reality you want for yourself. It is a journey that requires self-awareness, goal-setting, action, a positive mindset, and a commitment to personal growth and making a difference in the world.

One key aspect of living an empowered life is learning to trust yourself and your abilities. This means having confidence in your decisions and not second-guessing yourself. It means being true to yourself, even when faced with criticism or opposition from others. Trusting yourself also means being willing to take risks and step out of your comfort zone. By taking risks, you will be faced with new challenges and will have the opportunity to learn and grow as a person.

Another important aspect of living an empowered life is developing a strong sense of self-worth. This means recognizing your own value and understanding that you are worthy of love, respect, and happiness. It means not allowing others to define your worth or value, and instead, taking ownership of your own self-worth.

In addition to self-worth, living an empowered life also means developing a strong sense of self-care. This means taking care of your physical, emotional, and mental well-being. It means making time for yourself and engaging in activities that bring you joy and fulfillment. It also means learning to set boundaries and saying no to things that don't align with your values or goals.

To live an empowered life, it's also important to surround yourself with positive people. Having a supportive community of friends and family can help provide encouragement, guidance and motivation on your journey. It's also important to surround yourself with people who inspire and empower you, who believe in you and your potential.

Living an empowered life also means being mindful of the way you communicate with others. This means being assertive, clear, and direct in your communication, and learning to speak your truth. It also means listening actively and being open-minded to the perspectives of others.

In conclusion, living an empowered life is about taking control of your own destiny, developing a strong sense of self-awareness, setting goals, taking action, having a positive mindset, and making a difference in the world. It's about being true to yourself and living in alignment with your values and what is most important to you. It requires personal growth and development, but also a strong sense of self-worth, self-care, and supportive community. Remember that it's a journey and not a destination and always strive to be the best version of yourself.

# Book 4 - Overcome Trauma

A Comprehensive Guide to Understanding, Healing and Moving Forward from Past Trauma and Adversity, Including Techniques for Processing Traumatic Memories, Building Resilience, and Finding Empowerment

# 01: Introduction: Understanding Trauma and Its Impact

Trauma is a complex and multi-faceted phenomenon that can have a significant impact on an individual's physical, emotional, and mental well-being. It can manifest in a variety of ways, from physical injuries and illnesses to emotional and psychological distress. Understanding trauma and its impact is essential for addressing and treating the effects of traumatic experiences.

Trauma is defined as an event or series of events that threaten an individual's sense of safety, security, and well-being. It can be caused by a wide range of experiences, including physical and sexual abuse, neglect, natural disasters, war, terrorism, and accidents. Trauma can also result from witnessing or being a part of a traumatic event, such as a car crash or a mass shooting.

One of the key characteristics of trauma is that it can have a profound and long-lasting impact on an individual's emotional and mental well-being. Trauma can lead to a wide range of symptoms, including anxiety, depression, post-traumatic stress disorder (PTSD), and other emotional and behavioral disorders. These symptoms can be debilitating and can significantly interfere with an individual's ability to function in their daily life.

The impact of trauma can also be felt in the body, as trauma can lead to physical symptoms such as chronic pain, headaches, and gastrointestinal problems. Trauma can also contribute to the development of certain illnesses, such as heart disease, diabetes, and cancer.

Trauma can also have a significant impact on an individual's relationships and interactions with others. Trauma can lead to feelings of isolation, mistrust, and fear, which can make it difficult for an individual to form and maintain healthy relationships. Trauma can also lead to difficulties in communication and intimacy, which can further contribute to feelings of isolation and loneliness.

It is important to note that not everyone who experiences a traumatic event will develop symptoms of trauma. Factors such as an individual's coping mechanisms, support system, and overall resilience can play a role in determining the severity and duration of the impact of trauma.

Treatment for trauma is essential for addressing and managing the symptoms and effects of traumatic experiences. Treatment options can include therapy, medication, and other forms of support, such as support groups and self-care practices. It is important to work with a qualified professional to determine the best course of treatment for an individual's specific needs and circumstances.

In conclusion, trauma is a complex and multi-faceted phenomenon that can have a significant impact on an individual's physical, emotional, and mental well-being. Understanding trauma and its impact is essential for addressing and treating the effects of traumatic experiences. With proper treatment, individuals can learn to manage their symptoms and move towards a healthier and more fulfilling life.

It is also important to understand that trauma can be experienced differently by different individuals and groups. For example, marginalized and oppressed populations may be more likely to experience traumatic events and may also face additional barriers to accessing appropriate care. This highlights the importance of a culturally competent and trauma-informed approach to treating and supporting individuals who have experienced trauma.

Additionally, it is important to recognize that trauma can be intergenerational, meaning that the effects of trauma can be passed down through families and communities. This is particularly relevant in the case of historical trauma, such as the trauma experienced by Indigenous communities as a result of colonization and forced assimilation. Understanding the role of intergenerational trauma can be important in addressing and treating the effects of trauma.

In working with individuals who have experienced trauma, it is important to approach them with empathy, understanding, and non-judgment. Trauma can be a sensitive and difficult topic to discuss, and it is important to create a safe and supportive environment for individuals to share their experiences and feelings.

It is also important to recognize that healing from trauma is a process, and it may take time for an individual to fully recover. It is not a one-time event but a journey that requires patience, compassion and support.

In conclusion, understanding trauma and its impact is essential for effectively addressing and supporting individuals who have experienced traumatic events. This includes understanding the unique ways in which trauma can affect different individuals and groups, as well as the role of intergenerational trauma. It also includes approaching individuals with empathy, understanding, and a non-judgmental attitude, and recognizing that healing is a journey that requires patience and support.

# 02: The Trauma Response and Its Effects on the Mind and Body

Trauma is a powerful and often debilitating experience that can affect a person's mind and body in a number of ways. The trauma response is the set of physical and psychological reactions that occur in the aftermath of a traumatic event, and it can have a significant impact on a person's overall well-being.

The mind and body are closely connected, and trauma can affect both in a number of ways. Trauma can cause a range of psychological symptoms, such as anxiety, depression, and post-traumatic stress disorder (PTSD). These conditions can be difficult to cope with and can have a profound impact on a person's quality of life.

Trauma can also affect the body in a number of ways. For example, it can cause physical symptoms such as headaches, stomachaches, and muscle tension. These symptoms can be caused by the release of stress hormones, such as cortisol, in response to the traumatic event. Additionally, trauma can also lead to sleep disturbances, which can further contribute to physical and psychological symptoms.

## 02: THE TRAUMA RESPONSE AND ITS EFFECTS ON THE MIND AND BODY

The trauma response can also have long-term effects on a person's mind and body. For example, people who experience trauma may be more susceptible to developing chronic health conditions, such as heart disease or diabetes. This is because the stress response can have a negative impact on the body's immune system, making it more vulnerable to illness.

Trauma can also have a significant impact on a person's relationships and social interactions. People who have experienced trauma may have difficulty trusting others, and may struggle to form close relationships. This can lead to feelings of isolation and loneliness, which can further contribute to mental health problems.

There are a number of treatments available for people who have experienced trauma. One of the most effective is cognitive-behavioral therapy (CBT), which can help people to understand and cope with the thoughts and feelings that are associated with the trauma. Other therapies, such as eye movement desensitization and reprocessing (EMDR) and prolonged exposure therapy (PE), can also be helpful in treating trauma.

Medication can also be used to help people cope with the symptoms of trauma. Antidepressant medications, such as selective serotonin reuptake inhibitors (SSRIs), can be effective in treating depression and anxiety. Other medications, such as benzodiazepines, can be used to help people cope with insomnia and other sleep disturbances.

In addition to these treatments, it is also important for people who have experienced trauma to take care of themselves in other ways. This can include getting enough sleep, eating a healthy diet, and engaging in regular physical activity. This can help to reduce the physical symptoms of trauma and can also improve overall well-being.

In conclusion, trauma is a powerful and often debilitating experience that can affect a person's mind and body in a number of ways. The trauma response is the set of physical and psychological reactions that occur in the aftermath of a traumatic event, and it can have a significant impact on a person's overall well-being. There are a number of treatments available for people who have experienced trauma, including cognitive-behavioral therapy, eye movement desensitization and reprocessing and prolonged exposure therapy, medication and self-care practices. It is important for people who have experienced trauma to seek professional help and support so that they can cope with the symptoms of trauma and improve their overall well-being.

It is also important for individuals who have experienced trauma to have a support system in place. This can include family, friends, and support groups. Having people to talk to and share their experiences with can be a valuable source of comfort and understanding.

Another important aspect of trauma recovery is addressing any unresolved issues or traumas from the past. Trauma often has a ripple effect, and unresolved past traumas can contribute to the development of new traumas. By addressing these past traumas and resolving them, individuals can reduce the likelihood of developing new traumas or experiencing a re-traumatization.

It is also important to note that the trauma response and recovery process are unique to each individual. Some people may recover more quickly than others and some may have more severe symptoms. It is important to understand that recovery is not a linear process and that individuals may experience setbacks or relapses.

In summary, the trauma response and its effects on the mind and body can be severe and long-lasting. However, with the right treatment and support, individuals can learn to cope with the symptoms of trauma and improve their overall well-being. It is important for individuals who have experienced trauma to seek professional help and support, to build a support system, and to address any unresolved issues or past traumas. It's also important to understand that recovery is a unique process and should not be rushed or expect it to follow a linear pattern.

# 03: Types of Trauma and Adversity

Trauma and adversity come in many forms and can have a profound impact on an individual's mental and physical well-being. Understanding the different types of trauma and adversity can help in recognizing and addressing the effects they can have on a person's life.

One of the most commonly discussed types of trauma is that which arises from physical or sexual abuse. This can include both childhood and adult experiences of abuse, as well as domestic violence and sexual assault. The effects of abuse can be long-lasting and include symptoms such as depression, anxiety, and post-traumatic stress disorder (PTSD).

Another type of trauma that is often discussed is that which arises from experiencing or witnessing a traumatic event. This can include events such as natural disasters, terrorist attacks, or mass shootings. The effects of these types of trauma can also include symptoms such as depression, anxiety, and PTSD.

A less well-known but equally impactful type of trauma is that which arises from neglect or abandonment. This can include childhood experiences of neglect or abandonment by parents or caregivers, as well as neglect in adult relationships. The effects of neglect can include feelings of worthlessness, abandonment, and trust issues.

Adversity can also come in the form of chronic stressors such as poverty, discrimination, or long-term illness. These types of adversity can have a cumulative effect, leading to a range of mental and physical health problems.

Another type of adversity is vicarious trauma, which occurs when an individual is exposed to trauma through their work or occupation, such as a first responder, medical professional, or therapist. This can lead to symptoms of PTSD and other mental health issues.

It is important to note that not all individuals who experience trauma or adversity will develop mental health problems. However, it is important to be aware of the potential effects and to provide support and resources to those who may be struggling.

Treatment for trauma and adversity can include therapy, medication, and support groups. It's important to find a treatment approach that works best for the individual, as recovery and healing are unique to each person.

In conclusion, trauma and adversity come in many forms and can have a significant impact on an individual's well-being. Recognizing the different types of trauma and adversity and understanding the potential effects can help in providing support and resources to those who may be struggling. It is also important to remember that recovery and healing are unique to each person, and that a range of treatment options is available to support individuals in their journey towards healing.

Another important type of trauma to consider is complex trauma. This type of trauma occurs as a result of prolonged and repeated experiences of abuse, neglect, or other forms of maltreatment. This can include experiences such as growing up in a war-torn region or living in a chronically abusive household. The effects of complex trauma can be far-reaching and can include symptoms such as dissociation, self-harm, and difficulty forming healthy relationships.

Another type of trauma that is becoming increasingly recognized is developmental trauma. This type of trauma occurs as a result of disruptions or failures in the development of the brain and nervous system, which can occur due to adverse experiences in early childhood. This can include experiences such as neglect, abuse, or exposure to violence. The effects of developmental trauma can include difficulties with regulation of emotions and behavior, as well as difficulties with attachment and relationships.

Trauma and adversity can also occur as a result of a traumatic loss, such as the death of a loved one or the loss of a limb. This type of trauma can be incredibly difficult to process and can lead to symptoms of depression and grief.

Lastly, it's important to recognize that trauma and adversity can also occur within the context of one's culture or community. This can include experiences such as discrimination, racism, or cultural dislocation. The effects of this type of trauma can include feelings of alienation, cultural confusion and identity issues.

In summary, trauma and adversity can take on many forms, and it's important to consider the unique experiences of each individual. While some types of trauma are more well-known and discussed, such as physical and sexual abuse, other forms of trauma, such as complex trauma, developmental trauma, cultural trauma and traumatic loss, are equally impactful and deserve attention and support. It's crucial to understand the different types of trauma and adversity so that individuals can receive the appropriate support and resources to promote healing and recovery.

# 04: The Trauma Healing Process: Understanding the Stages of Recovery

Trauma is a deeply distressing or disturbing event that can have a lasting impact on an individual's mental, emotional, and physical well-being. The trauma healing process is a journey that can take time and requires patience, understanding, and support. It is important to understand that everyone's experience of trauma is unique and their healing journey will be different. However, there are some general stages of recovery that are commonly recognized in the trauma healing process.

The first stage of the trauma healing process is the acute stage. This stage is characterized by feelings of shock, disbelief, and numbness. The individual may have difficulty processing what has happened and may have trouble sleeping, eating, or engaging in daily activities. They may also experience physical symptoms such as headaches, muscle tension, and fatigue.

The second stage of the trauma healing process is the denial stage. This stage is characterized by a refusal to acknowledge or accept the reality of the trauma. The individual may try to deny that the trauma occurred or may minimize the impact it has had on their life. They may also try to avoid thinking or talking about the trauma.

The third stage of the trauma healing process is the anger stage. This stage is characterized by feelings of anger, resentment, and frustration. The individual may be angry at themselves, the perpetrator, or others who were involved in the trauma. They may also feel that the trauma is unfair or unjust.

The fourth stage of the trauma healing process is the bargaining stage. This stage is characterized by a feeling of helplessness and a desire to regain control. The individual may try to make deals with themselves or with a higher power in an attempt to undo or change the trauma. They may also try to find meaning in the trauma by searching for a lesson to be learned.

The fifth stage of the trauma healing process is the depression stage. This stage is characterized by feelings of sadness, hopelessness, and despair. The individual may have difficulty finding pleasure in things they used to enjoy and may have trouble sleeping or eating. They may also feel guilty, ashamed, or responsible for the trauma.

The sixth stage of the trauma healing process is the acceptance stage. This stage is characterized by a recognition and acceptance of the reality of the trauma. The individual may have a renewed sense of hope and may begin to move forward in their life. They may also begin to find new ways to cope with the trauma and to find meaning in their experience.

It's important to note that these stages are not linear, and a person may revisit different stages at different times or may not go through all of the stages. Additionally, some people may experience long-term psychological symptoms, such as post-traumatic stress disorder (PTSD) and may need additional support and treatment. It's also important to note that healing is a unique and personal process that may take different form for each individual.

In conclusion, the trauma healing process is a journey that can take time and requires patience, understanding, and support. It is important to understand that everyone's experience of trauma is unique and their healing journey will

be different. However, by understanding the stages of recovery, it can help individuals better understand their own
healing journey and provide them with the support they
need to move forward. It's also important to seek professional help if needed and never feel ashamed to reach out
for support.

It's also important to note that the trauma healing process
can be different for different individuals. Some people may
find traditional therapy, such as cognitive-behavioral therapy, to be helpful in their healing journey. Others may find
alternative therapies, such as art therapy or mindfulness-
based practices, to be more beneficial. It's important for individuals to explore different options and find what works
best for them.

Another important aspect of the trauma healing process is
self-care. Taking care of oneself physically, emotionally, and
mentally is crucial in the healing process. This may include
things such as exercise, healthy eating, getting enough
sleep, and engaging in activities that bring joy and relaxation. It's also important to practice self-compassion and be
kind to oneself during this journey.

## 04: THE TRAUMA HEALING PROCESS: UNDERSTAND-
## ING THE STAGES OF RECOVERY

It's important to remember that healing from trauma is not a one-time event. It's a continuous process that may take time, and individuals may experience setbacks along the way. It's important to be patient with oneself and to recognize that healing is not a linear process. It's also important to understand that healing is not the same as forgetting or erasing the trauma. It's about learning to live with the trauma and finding ways to cope with it.

In addition to individual therapy and self-care, support from friends, family, and loved ones is an important aspect of the trauma healing process. Having people to talk to and share the journey with can be incredibly helpful. It's also important for loved ones to be patient and understanding during the healing process, as well as educate themselves about trauma and its effects.

In conclusion, the trauma healing process is a journey that takes time, patience, and support. It's important to understand that everyone's experience of trauma is unique and their healing journey will be different. However, by understanding the stages of recovery, exploring different therapy options, practicing self-care and having a support system, individuals can find ways to heal and move forward in their lives. Remember that healing is not a one-time event, it's an ongoing process and it's important to be kind to yourself and to seek help if needed.

# 05: The Importance of Self-Care in Trauma Recovery

Self-care is a critical component of the healing process for individuals who have experienced trauma. Trauma can take many forms, from physical abuse to emotional neglect, and can have a profound impact on an individual's mental and physical well-being. The effects of trauma can be long-lasting and can manifest in a variety of ways, including depression, anxiety, and post-traumatic stress disorder (PTSD).

Self-care is a way for individuals to take control of their own healing and to actively work towards recovery. It involves engaging in activities that promote physical and mental well-being, such as exercise, healthy eating, and stress-management techniques. It also includes taking time for oneself, setting boundaries, and learning to say no to demands that may be overwhelming.

One of the most important aspects of self-care is understanding and acknowledging the impact of trauma on one's life. This means being honest with oneself about the ways in which trauma has affected one's thoughts, feelings, and behaviors. It also means acknowledging the impact of trauma on relationships and recognizing the need for support from others.

Self-care also involves learning to cope with the symptoms of trauma, such as flashbacks and nightmares. This can be done through a variety of methods, such as cognitive-behavioral therapy, mindfulness techniques, and medication. In addition, self-care includes taking steps to manage stress and to build resilience, such as exercise, yoga, and meditation.

Self-care also involves learning to set boundaries and to take time for oneself. This means saying no to demands that may be overwhelming and setting limits on the amount of time and energy one is willing to give to others. It also means learning to set boundaries with oneself, such as setting realistic goals and taking time to rest and relax.

Self-care also involves taking care of one's physical health. This includes getting enough sleep, eating a healthy diet, and engaging in regular physical activity. It also means paying attention to physical symptoms that may be related to trauma and seeking medical attention when necessary.

Finally, self-care involves reaching out for help and support when needed. This may include talking to a therapist or counselor, joining a support group, or talking to friends and family. It is important to remember that healing from trauma is a process and that it is not something that can be done alone.

In conclusion, self-care is an essential component of trauma recovery. It involves taking control of one's own healing, acknowledging the impact of trauma, learning to cope with symptoms, setting boundaries, taking care of one's physical health, and reaching out for help and support. It is a ongoing process of self-discovery and self-care that is essential for individuals who have experienced trauma to live a fulfilling life.

Self-care is not a one-time event, but a continuous process that requires ongoing effort and commitment. It is important to remember that healing from trauma is not a linear process and that there will be setbacks and challenges along the way. It is important to be patient with oneself and to recognize that progress may be slow.

It is also important to recognize that self-care is not just about taking care of oneself, but also about understanding

and addressing the societal and cultural factors that contribute to trauma. For example, recognizing and addressing
the impact of racism, poverty, and discrimination on mental
health and well-being is an important aspect of self-care for
marginalized communities.

In order to practice self-care, it is important to make a plan
and to set achievable goals. This may include setting aside
time each day for self-care activities, such as exercise or
meditation, or setting a goal to attend a certain number of
therapy sessions each month. It may also include making a
list of self-care activities that are enjoyable and meaningful,
such as reading a book or taking a relaxing bath.

It is also important to be mindful of self-care practices that
may be harmful or unproductive, such as substance abuse
or avoiding responsibilities. These practices may provide
temporary relief, but they ultimately perpetuate the negative effects of trauma and can lead to further harm in the
long run.

In addition, self-care also includes seeking professional
help, such as counseling or therapy, when needed. A trained
therapist can help individuals understand and cope with the

effects of trauma, as well as provide tools and strategies for self-care and healing.

In conclusion, self-care is an essential aspect of the healing process for individuals who have experienced trauma. It involves acknowledging the impact of trauma, learning to cope with symptoms, setting boundaries, taking care of one's physical health, and reaching out for help and support. It is a ongoing process of self-discovery and self-care that requires patience, effort, and commitment. Additionally, it is important to recognize the societal and cultural factors that contribute to trauma and to address them. Remember that healing is a journey, and it is not something that can be rushed or forced, but rather it is something that one should take the time to nurture and care for.

# 06: Processing Traumatic Memories: Techniques and Strategies

Traumatic memories can have a significant impact on an individual's mental health and well-being. These memories are often vivid, distressing, and can be triggered by seemingly insignificant cues in the individual's environment. Processing traumatic memories is an essential step in healing and moving forward. In this chapter, we will discuss techniques and strategies for processing traumatic memories.

One of the most effective techniques for processing traumatic memories is cognitive-behavioral therapy (CBT). CBT is a form of psychotherapy that focuses on the relationship between thoughts, feelings, and behaviors. The goal of CBT is to help individuals identify and change negative thought patterns and beliefs that may be preventing them from moving on from their traumatic experiences.

One technique used in CBT is exposure therapy. Exposure therapy involves gradually confronting the traumatic memories in a controlled and safe environment. The individual will be asked to describe their traumatic memory in detail, including their thoughts and feelings at the time. The

therapist will then help the individual challenge any negative thoughts and beliefs that may be associated with the
memory. Over time, as the individual becomes more comfortable with the memory, they will be able to think about it
without feeling overwhelmed.

Another technique used in CBT is cognitive restructuring.
This technique involves identifying and challenging negative thoughts and beliefs associated with the traumatic
memory. The individual will be asked to identify their automatic thoughts and beliefs and to challenge them with more
realistic and balanced thoughts. This can help the individual
to see the traumatic event in a different light and to develop
a more positive perspective.

A different strategy is Eye Movement Desensitization and
Reprocessing (EMDR). EMDR is a form of psychotherapy
that uses bilateral stimulation, such as eye movements, to
process traumatic memories. The therapist will guide the
individual to recall their traumatic memory while engaging
in the bilateral stimulation. The theory is that the bilateral
stimulation helps to process the traumatic memory, making
it less distressing.

Another strategy is Mindfulness-based therapy. Mindfulness-based therapy involves learning to be present in the moment and to focus on one's thoughts and feelings without judgment. This can help individuals to become more aware of their thoughts and feelings and to develop a sense of acceptance and understanding. Mindfulness-based therapy can be used in conjunction with other techniques to help individuals process traumatic memories.

Another strategy is Relaxation techniques. Relaxation techniques such as deep breathing, progressive muscle relaxation, and visualization can help individuals to reduce their emotional distress and physical tension. Relaxation techniques can be used to help individuals calm down when they are feeling overwhelmed by traumatic memories.

It's important to note that processing traumatic memories can be a difficult and emotional process, and it's important to have a support system in place. This may include friends, family, or a therapist. It's also important to remember that healing is a process and it may take time.

In conclusion, processing traumatic memories is an important step in healing and moving forward. There are various

techniques and strategies that can be used to help individuals process traumatic memories, including cognitive-behavioral therapy, exposure therapy, cognitive restructuring,
Eye Movement Desensitization and Reprocessing, mindfulness-based therapy and relaxation techniques. It's important to work with a therapist or counselor and to have a support system in place while processing traumatic memories.
Remember to be patient and compassionate with yourself as
healing can take time.

Another strategy for processing traumatic memories is to
use creative outlets such as art, writing, or music. These
outlets can provide a way for individuals to express their
thoughts and feelings about their traumatic experiences
without the need for words. This can be especially helpful
for individuals who may have difficulty verbalizing their
thoughts and feelings.

Art therapy, for example, is a form of therapy that uses art
materials such as paint, clay, or collage to help individuals
express their thoughts and feelings. The therapist will guide
the individual to create art that represents their traumatic
experience, and will then help the individual to explore

their thoughts and feelings about the art.

Writing therapy, also known as journaling, is a form of therapy that involves writing about one's thoughts and feelings. The therapist will guide the individual to write about their traumatic experience, and will then help the individual to explore their thoughts and feelings about the experience.

Music therapy is a form of therapy that uses music to help individuals express their thoughts and feelings. The therapist will guide the individual to listen to music that represents their traumatic experience, and will then help the individual to explore their thoughts and feelings about the music.

It's important to note that these creative outlets should be used in conjunction with other techniques, such as cognitive-behavioral therapy or exposure therapy. They can be an additional tool to help individuals process their traumatic memories.

In addition to the above strategies, it's also important to take care of oneself while processing traumatic memories. This includes getting enough sleep, eating a healthy diet, and engaging in regular physical activity. These self-care practices can help to reduce stress and promote overall well-being.

In conclusion, processing traumatic memories is a difficult but necessary process in order to move forward and heal. There are various techniques and strategies that can be used to help individuals process traumatic memories, such as cognitive-behavioral therapy, exposure therapy, cognitive restructuring, Eye Movement Desensitization and Reprocessing, mindfulness-based therapy, relaxation techniques, and creative outlets such as art, writing, and music therapy. It's important to work with a therapist or counselor and to have a support system in place while processing traumatic memories. Additionally, self-care practices such as getting enough sleep, eating a healthy diet, and engaging in regular physical activity can also play an important role in promoting overall well-being. Remember to be patient and compassionate with yourself as healing can take time.

# 07: Building Resilience: How to Develop a Stronger Mind and Spirit

Building resilience is the ability to bounce back from adversity and to maintain a positive outlook in the face of difficult circumstances. It is a combination of mental, emotional, and physical strength that enables individuals to cope with stress and adversity, and to emerge from difficult situations stronger and more capable than before. Resilience is an important skill to develop, as it can help you to overcome challenges and to live a more fulfilling life.

There are several key strategies that you can use to develop resilience and to build a stronger mind and spirit. These strategies include:

– Setting realistic goals: Setting realistic goals is one of the most effective ways to build resilience. When you set goals that are achievable and that align with your values, you are more likely to feel motivated and energized by the process of working towards them. This can help you to maintain a positive outlook and to persevere through difficult times.

– Practicing mindfulness: Mindfulness is the practice of being present in the moment and paying attention to your thoughts, feelings, and sensations without judgment. It can help you to develop resilience by enabling you to stay focused on the present moment and to avoid getting bogged down by negative thoughts and emotions.

– Building a support network: Building a support network of friends, family, and professionals can help you to build resilience by providing you with a sense of connection and belonging. When you feel supported, you are more likely to feel confident and capable of facing challenges.

– Engaging in physical activity: Engaging in regular physical activity is one of the most effective ways to build resilience. Exercise releases endorphins, which are chemicals that can make you feel happier and more energized. Additionally, regular exercise can help to improve your overall physical health, which can in turn help to boost your mental and emotional well-being.

– Fostering a positive attitude: Fostering a positive attitude is one of the most effective ways to build resilience. When you focus on the good things in your life and practice gratitude, you are more likely to feel positive and optimistic about your future. Additionally, when you practice positive thinking, you can help to counteract the negative thoughts and emotions that can hold you back.

– Give back to community and help others: Giving back to community and helping others can help to build resilience by providing a sense of purpose and meaning. When you are able to make a positive impact on the world, you are more likely to feel fulfilled and satisfied with your life. Additionally, helping others can take the focus off of your own problems, which can help to reduce stress and anxiety.

In conclusion, building resilience is an ongoing process that requires time and effort, but the benefits are well worth it. By setting realistic goals, practicing mindfulness, building a support network, engaging in physical activity, fostering a positive attitude and giving back to community, you can develop a stronger mind and spirit that will help you to cope with stress and adversity, and to live a more fulfilling life. Remember that resilience is not about never experiencing difficulties, it's about being able to handle them and find the opportunities in them.

– Learning from failure: Failure is an inevitable part of life, and it is important to learn from it rather than dwelling on it. When you fail, it is important to take the time to reflect on what went wrong and what you can do differently next time. This can help you to build resilience by teaching you valuable lessons and helping you to grow as a person.

– Developing a growth mindset: Having a growth mindset means embracing challenges and seeing them as opportunities for growth. When you have a growth mindset, you are more likely to take risks and to view failure as a learning opportunity. This can help you to build resilience by teaching you to be more adaptable and to view challenges as opportunities for growth.

– Taking care of yourself: Taking care of yourself is crucial for building resilience. This means taking care of your physical, emotional and mental health. Eating a healthy diet, getting enough sleep, practicing self-care and managing stress are all important for maintaining good overall health.

– Seek professional help when needed: If you are struggling to build resilience on your own, it may be helpful to seek professional help. A therapist or counselor can help you to work through difficult emotions and to develop strategies for coping with stress and adversity. They can also help you to identify and address any underlying issues that may be contributing to your difficulties.

In conclusion, building resilience is a lifelong process that requires time and effort, but the benefits are well worth it. By setting realistic goals, practicing mindfulness, building a support network, engaging in physical activity, fostering a positive attitude, giving back to community, learning from failure, developing a growth mindset, taking care of yourself and seeking professional help when needed, you can develop a stronger mind and spirit that will help you to cope with stress and adversity, and to live a more fulfilling life. Remember that resilience is not about never experiencing difficulties, it's about being able to handle them and find the opportunities in them.

# 08: Finding Empowerment: How to Take Control of Your Trauma Narrative

Introduction

Trauma can be a devastating and debilitating experience, leaving those who have gone through it feeling lost, alone, and without control. However, it is possible to take control of your trauma narrative and find empowerment in the aftermath. This chapter will explore some of the ways you can take control of your trauma narrative, including understanding your trauma, facing your feelings, and finding support.

Understanding Your Trauma

The first step to taking control of your trauma narrative is to understand what trauma is and how it has affected you. Trauma is a deeply distressing or disturbing event that can have lasting effects on a person's mental, emotional, and physical well-being. It can be caused by a variety of events, such as physical or emotional abuse, sexual assault, natural disasters, or the loss of a loved one.

## 08: FINDING EMPOWERMENT: HOW TO TAKE CONTROL OF YOUR TRAUMA NARRATIVE

It is important to understand that everyone's experience of trauma is unique, and there is no "right" or "wrong" way to feel. You may feel a range of emotions, including anger, fear, guilt, and sadness. You may also experience physical symptoms such as headaches, fatigue, and difficulty sleeping. It is important to acknowledge and accept these feelings, rather than trying to push them away or ignore them.

Facing Your Feelings

Once you have a better understanding of your trauma and how it has affected you, it is important to face your feelings head-on. This may mean talking to a therapist or counselor, writing in a journal, or talking to a trusted friend or family member. It is important to find a way to express your feelings that feels safe and comfortable for you.

It is also important to remember that healing is a process, and it may take time. You may have setbacks, and that's okay. It's important to be patient with yourself and to remember that you are not alone in your journey.

Finding Support

## 08: FINDING EMPOWERMENT: HOW TO TAKE CONTROL OF YOUR TRAUMA NARRATIVE

One of the most important things you can do to take control of your trauma narrative is to find support. This can come in many forms, including therapy, counseling, support groups, or even online communities. It is important to find a support system that feels safe and comfortable for you.

It is also important to surround yourself with people who understand and support you. This may mean cutting ties with people who are not supportive or who may be triggering to you. It is important to remember that you deserve to be surrounded by people who care about you and want to help you heal.

Conclusion

Taking control of your trauma narrative can be a difficult and challenging process, but it is possible. By understanding your trauma, facing your feelings, and finding support, you can begin to take control of your story and find empowerment in the aftermath. Remember to be patient with yourself, and to surround yourself with people who care about you and want to help you heal. With time and support, you can come to a place of peace and acceptance.

## 08: FINDING EMPOWERMENT: HOW TO TAKE CON-TROL OF YOUR TRAUMA NARRATIVE

Another important aspect of taking control of your trauma narrative is to learn how to manage and cope with the symptoms that may result from your trauma. This may include things like anxiety, depression, and flashbacks. It is important to educate yourself about these symptoms and to learn ways to manage them. This can include things like mindfulness techniques, cognitive-behavioral therapy, and medication. It is also important to find a support system that can help you manage your symptoms, whether that be a therapist, counselor, or support group.

Another important aspect of taking control of your trauma narrative is to find ways to take care of yourself. Self-care is crucial for healing, and it can include things like exercise, eating a healthy diet, getting enough sleep, and engaging in activities that you enjoy. It is also important to find ways to relax and de-stress, such as yoga, meditation, or listening to music.

In addition, it's important to be open to the idea of forgiveness, both for yourself and for others. Forgiveness is not about forgetting or excusing the hurt that was done, but it's about accepting that it happened, and not allowing it to continue to control you. It is a process and it can take time, but it is worth it in the end.

Finally, it is important to remember that you are not defined by your trauma. You are not a victim, you are a survivor. You have the strength and resilience to overcome what you have been through, and to live a fulfilling and meaningful life. You are capable of finding empowerment and taking control of your trauma narrative.

In conclusion, Finding empowerment after a traumatic event is a journey and it can be hard and take time, but it is important to understand your trauma, to face your feelings, to find support and to learn how to cope with the symptoms that may result from your trauma, to take care of yourself, to learn forgiveness, and to remember that you are not defined by your trauma. With time and support, you can come to a place of peace and acceptance and start to take control of your narrative and empower yourself.

# 09: Navigating Support Systems: Finding Help and Resources

Navigating Support Systems: Finding Help and Resources

When dealing with difficult situations, it can be overwhelming to try and find the right resources and support. Whether you are facing a personal crisis, dealing with mental health issues, or trying to navigate the healthcare system, it can be hard to know where to turn for help. In this chapter, we will explore some strategies for finding the support and resources you need to get through tough times.

First, it is important to understand that there is no one-size-fits-all solution when it comes to finding support. Different people may need different types of help and resources depending on their specific situation. However, there are some general tips and strategies that can be helpful when trying to find the right support for you.

One important strategy is to do your research. There are many different types of support and resources available, so it can be helpful to take the time to learn about the different options that are available. This can include things like therapy, support groups, and healthcare services. By researching different options, you can get a better sense of what might be the best fit for your needs.

Another important strategy is to reach out to people you trust. This can include friends, family members, and other loved ones who can provide you with emotional support and guidance. They may also be able to provide you with information about different resources and support systems that they have used in the past.

You can also seek out professional help. You can talk to a therapist, counselor, or other mental health professional who can provide you with guidance and support. They can help you work through your feelings and develop coping strategies that can help you get through difficult times. They can also help you navigate the healthcare system and find the right resources for your needs.

Additionally, many organizations, such as non-profits and government agencies, provide a wide range of services and support to those who need it. You can contact these organizations directly and ask about the services they offer. They can provide you with information about programs and services that may be able to help you.

In addition, many communities have helplines that provide a wide range of support services and resources. They can provide you with information about local services and resources and connect you with the right people who can help.

It is also important to know your rights. This can include understanding your rights as a patient and your rights to access healthcare services and other types of support. Knowing your rights can help you advocate for yourself and get the help you need.

Finally, it is important to remember that you are not alone. There are many people who are going through similar situations and who have been able to find the support and resources they need to get through tough times. It may take some time and effort to find the right resources and support, but with persistence and determination, you can get the help you need.

In conclusion, finding the right support and resources can be a challenging task, but with the right strategies, you can navigate the support systems and find the help you need. It is important to do your research, reach out to people you trust, seek professional help, and know your rights. Remember that you are not alone and that with persistence, you can get the help you need to get through difficult times.

It's also important to be open to trying different types of support and resources. What works for one person may not work for another, so it's important to be willing to try different options and find what works best for you. This may include therapy, medication, support groups, and other types of resources.

Another important aspect of navigating support systems is being aware of cultural and language barriers. If English is not your first language, or if you come from a different cultural background, it may be difficult to find resources and support that are tailored to your specific needs. In this case, it may be helpful to seek out resources and support that are culturally and linguistically appropriate. This may include organizations that serve specific ethnic and linguistic communities or translation services that can help you communicate with healthcare providers and other types of support.

It's also important to be aware of financial barriers when seeking help and resources. Many support systems and resources require payment, and this can be a barrier for some people. If you are unable to afford the support or resources you need, it may be helpful to seek out organizations that provide financial assistance or programs that can help you pay for the support and resources you need.

Finally, it's important to remember that seeking help and resources is not a sign of weakness. It takes courage and strength to admit that you need help, and it's important to remember that everyone goes through difficult times and needs support. Seeking help and resources is a sign of resilience and the determination to improve your well-being.

In conclusion, navigating support systems can be a challenging task, but with the right strategies and information, you can find the help and resources you need to get through difficult times. It's important to do your research, reach out to people you trust, seek professional help, and know your rights. Remember to be open to trying different types of support, be aware of cultural and language barriers, and financial barriers, and remember that seeking help is a sign of strength and resilience.

# 10: Trauma and Relationships: How Trauma Can Affect Connections with Others

Trauma can have a profound impact on an individual's ability to form and maintain healthy relationships. Traumatic experiences, such as physical or emotional abuse, neglect, or exposure to violence, can disrupt the development of secure attachment patterns, affect the way a person sees themselves and others, and influence the way they cope with stress and negative emotions. As a result, trauma survivors may struggle to trust, communicate effectively, and form intimate connections with others.

One of the most significant ways that trauma can affect relationships is through the development of insecure attachment patterns. Secure attachment patterns develop when a child feels safe and secure in their relationship with their primary caregiver, and as a result, they learn to trust and rely on others. However, when a child experiences trauma, such as abuse or neglect, they may learn that the people they depend on for survival are not trustworthy or safe. As a result, they may develop insecure attachment patterns, such as avoidant or anxious attachment styles.

Individuals with avoidant attachment styles tend to avoid intimacy and close relationships, often pushing people away to protect themselves from potential hurt or rejection. They may have difficulty trusting others and may struggle to form deep emotional connections. On the other hand, individuals with anxious attachment styles may crave intimacy and close relationships, but may struggle to trust others and may have difficulty setting healthy boundaries. They may also experience intense feelings of insecurity and fear of abandonment.

Trauma can also affect the way a person sees themselves and others. Trauma survivors may develop negative self-perceptions, such as feeling guilty, ashamed, or worthless. They may also struggle to trust their own perceptions and may doubt their ability to make healthy decisions. As a result, they may have difficulty setting healthy boundaries and may struggle to assert themselves in relationships.

Additionally, trauma can influence the way a person copes with stress and negative emotions. Trauma survivors may develop unhealthy coping mechanisms, such as substance abuse, self-harm, or avoidance. These coping mechanisms can interfere with the ability to form and maintain healthy relationships. For example, substance abuse can lead to problems with communication, trust, and intimacy, while avoidance can interfere with the ability to resolve conflicts and work through problems.

Furthermore, trauma can also lead to the development of certain mental health conditions, such as PTSD or depression, which can further affect relationships. Symptoms of PTSD, such as flashbacks and hypervigilance, can make it difficult for the person to relax and feel safe in close relationships. Depression can lead to feelings of worthlessness, hopelessness and lack of energy, making it hard for the person to engage in social interactions and maintain relationships.

It's important to note that trauma can affect different people in different ways and it's not possible to predict how someone will react to traumatic events. However, there are several ways to help individuals who have experienced trauma to build and maintain healthy relationships. One of the most effective ways is through therapy, such as cognitive-behavioral therapy, which can help individuals to identify and challenge negative thoughts and beliefs, develop healthy coping mechanisms, and improve communication skills.

Another effective way is through trauma-focused therapy, such as Eye Movement Desensitization and Reprocessing (EMDR) which aims to process and heal traumatic memories, so the person can live a life that is less affected by traumatic memories. Trauma-focused therapy can also help individuals to develop a sense of safety, trust, and connection with others.

It's important for the person's support system, family, and friends to be understanding and supportive of the person's healing process. It's also important for them to educate themselves about trauma and its effects on relationships, in order to provide the right kind of support.

In conclusion, trauma can have a significant impact on an individual's ability to form and maintain healthy relationships. Trauma survivors may struggle with trust, communication, and intimacy due to the development of insecure attachment patterns, negative self-perceptions, and unhealthy coping mechanisms. Additionally, trauma can also lead to the development of certain mental health conditions, such as PTSD or depression, which can further affect relationships.

However, there are ways to help individuals who have experienced trauma to build and maintain healthy relationships. Therapy, such as cognitive-behavioral therapy and trauma-focused therapy, can help individuals to identify and challenge negative thoughts and beliefs, develop healthy coping mechanisms, and improve communication skills. It's also important for the person's support system, family, and friends to be understanding and supportive of the person's healing process and educate themselves about trauma and its effects on relationships.

It's essential to remember that healing and recovery from trauma is a process and it takes time. It's important to be patient and compassionate with oneself and others who have experienced trauma, and to keep in mind that healing and forming healthy relationships is possible.

# 11: Trauma and Mental Health: Understanding the Connection

Trauma and mental health are closely connected, as experiences of trauma can have a profound impact on an individual's mental well-being. Trauma refers to a wide range of experiences, including physical and emotional abuse, neglect, natural disasters, and military combat. The effects of trauma can be long-lasting and can manifest in a variety of ways, including anxiety, depression, and post-traumatic stress disorder (PTSD).

When an individual experiences a traumatic event, their brain and body respond in a way that is designed to protect them from harm. The body's "fight or flight" response is activated, releasing hormones such as adrenaline and cortisol that help the individual respond to the threat. This response can be helpful in the immediate aftermath of a traumatic event, as it allows the individual to take action to protect themselves. However, if the trauma is not resolved, the individual may continue to experience the symptoms of this response, such as increased heart rate, difficulty sleeping, and difficulty concentrating.

For some individuals, the effects of trauma may not become

apparent until weeks, months, or even years after the event. This is particularly true for individuals who have experienced complex trauma, such as ongoing abuse or neglect. Complex trauma is characterized by repeated and prolonged exposure to traumatic events, and it can have a particularly devastating impact on an individual's mental health.

One of the most common mental health conditions associated with trauma is PTSD. This condition is characterized by a range of symptoms, including intrusive thoughts or memories of the traumatic event, avoidance of people, places, or activities that remind the individual of the trauma, and feelings of hypervigilance or increased arousal. Individuals with PTSD may also experience flashbacks or nightmares, and they may feel detached or emotionally numb.

Another common condition that can develop as a result of trauma is depression. Trauma can be a significant risk factor for the development of depression, and individuals who have experienced trauma may be more likely to experience feelings of hopelessness, helplessness, and worthlessness. They may also have difficulty sleeping, lose interest in activities that they once enjoyed, and have difficulty concentrating.

Anxiety disorders are also commonly associated with trauma. Trauma can cause individuals to feel constantly on edge, and they may experience physical symptoms such as a racing heart or difficulty breathing. They may also experience feelings of panic and fear, and they may avoid certain people, places, or activities that remind them of the trauma.

In addition to these specific mental health conditions, trauma can also impact an individual's overall well-being. Individuals who have experienced trauma may have difficulty trusting others, and they may have difficulty forming and maintaining healthy relationships. They may also have difficulty regulating their emotions, and they may experience feelings of shame or guilt.

It's important to note that not everyone who experiences trauma will develop mental health problems. Resilience and support from loved ones and mental health professionals can play a key role in helping individuals to cope with the effects of trauma. However, for many individuals, professional help is necessary to process and heal from the trauma.

Treatment for trauma-related mental health conditions typically involves talk therapy, such as cognitive-behavioral therapy (CBT) or eye movement desensitization and reprocessing (EMDR). These therapies can help individuals to process their traumatic experiences, learn to manage their symptoms, and develop coping strategies. Medications, such as antidepressants, may also be prescribed to help manage symptoms of depression and anxiety.

In conclusion, trauma and mental health are closely connected, and experiences of trauma can have a profound impact on an individual's mental well-being. Trauma can lead to a wide range of mental health problems, including PTSD, depression, and anxiety disorders. It's important to for individuals who have experienced trauma to receive professional help in order to process and heal from their experiences. Treatment for trauma-related mental health conditions typically involves talk therapy and medication, and can help individuals to manage their symptoms and develop coping strategies. It's also important for individuals, friends and families to understand the connection between trauma and mental health, in order to recognize the symptoms and seek help early on.

Additionally, it's important to address the societal and systemic issues that can lead to trauma, such as poverty, discrimination, and lack of access to resources. Addressing these issues can help to reduce the prevalence of trauma and improve mental health outcomes for individuals and communities.

It's important to remember that healing from trauma is a process, and it can take time. But with the right support and resources, individuals can learn to manage their symptoms and move forward in their lives. It's important to be patient with yourself and to seek help if you're struggling with the effects of trauma.

# 12: Trauma and Addiction: How Trauma Can Lead to Substance Abuse

Trauma and addiction are closely intertwined. Trauma can lead to substance abuse as a way of coping with overwhelming emotions and memories. Conversely, substance abuse can also lead to further trauma, creating a cycle that can be difficult to break. In this chapter, we will explore the relationship between trauma and addiction and how understanding this connection can aid in the treatment of both conditions.

Trauma is defined as a deeply distressing or disturbing experience that can have long-lasting effects on an individual's mental and physical well-being. Examples of trauma include experiencing or witnessing violence, natural disasters, sexual or physical abuse, and accidents. Trauma can also be cumulative, resulting from multiple small events that add up over time.

When an individual experiences trauma, it can have a profound impact on their mental and emotional state. They may experience symptoms such as anxiety, depression, and flashbacks, which can make it difficult to function in daily life. Trauma can also disrupt the body's stress response, leading to chronic physical symptoms such as headaches, chronic pain, and stomach problems.

Substance abuse, on the other hand, is the use of drugs or alcohol in a way that is harmful to the individual or those around them. This can include using a substance in a way that is not medically prescribed, using a substance for longer than intended, or using a substance despite knowing it is causing problems in their life. Substance abuse can lead to addiction, a chronic brain disease characterized by compulsive drug-seeking and use despite the harmful consequences.

The relationship between trauma and substance abuse is complex and multifaceted. Trauma can lead to substance abuse as a way of coping with the overwhelming emotions and memories associated with the traumatic event. Drugs and alcohol can provide temporary relief from these symptoms, leading the individual to use them more frequently and eventually becoming addicted.

Additionally, individuals who have experienced trauma are

more likely to develop substance abuse problems than those who have not. Studies have shown that individuals who have experienced traumatic events are at a higher risk of developing substance abuse problems, with the risk increasing with the number of traumatic events experienced.

Substance abuse can also lead to further trauma. For example, individuals who are under the influence of drugs or alcohol may be more likely to be involved in accidents or violent incidents. Additionally, individuals who are addicted to drugs or alcohol may experience financial, legal, and relationship problems, which can also be traumatic.

Understanding the relationship between trauma and addiction is crucial in treating both conditions. Trauma-informed care is an approach that recognizes the impact of trauma and incorporates this understanding into the treatment process. This approach recognizes that individuals who have experienced trauma may have different needs and may require a different approach than those who have not.

Treatment for substance abuse typically includes a combination of therapy and medication. Therapy can include cognitive-behavioral therapy, which helps individuals identify and change negative thought patterns and behaviors associated with substance abuse. Medication-assisted treatment (MAT) can also be effective in treating substance abuse, particularly for individuals addicted to opioids.

Trauma-specific therapies, such as eye movement desensitization and reprocessing (EMDR) or prolonged exposure therapy, can also be effective in treating the symptoms of trauma. These therapies help individuals process and make sense of the traumatic event, reducing the emotional impact and allowing them to move forward.

In conclusion, trauma and addiction are closely intertwined and understanding the relationship between the two can aid in the treatment of both conditions. Trauma can lead to substance abuse as a way of coping with overwhelming emotions and memories. Substance abuse can also lead to further trauma, creating a cycle that can be difficult to break. Trauma-informed care, which recognizes the impact of trauma and incorporates this understanding into the treatment process, is crucial in treating both trauma and addiction. It is important to address both conditions simultaneously, as one can exacerbate the other.

## 12: TRAUMA AND ADDICTION: HOW TRAUMA CAN LEAD TO SUBSTANCE ABUSE

It is also important to note that not all individuals who have experienced trauma will develop substance abuse problems, and not all individuals who struggle with substance abuse have a history of trauma. However, recognizing the potential connection between the two can aid in providing more comprehensive and effective treatment.

In addition to therapy and medication, other supportive measures such as self-care practices, mindfulness, and support groups can be beneficial in the treatment of trauma and addiction. A holistic approach that addresses physical, emotional, and social well-being can help individuals develop the skills and resilience to cope with difficult emotions and memories, and ultimately break the cycle of trauma and addiction.

It is important to remember that recovery from trauma and addiction is a journey, and it may take time for individuals to heal and recover. It is important to provide support and encouragement throughout the process and to remember that everyone's journey is unique. With the right approach and support, individuals can overcome the trauma and addiction and move forward towards a healthier and more ful-

# 12: TRAUMA AND ADDICTION: HOW TRAUMA CAN LEAD TO SUBSTANCE ABUSE

filling life.

# 13: Trauma and the Workplace: How Trauma Can Affect Your Career

Trauma is a deeply distressing or disturbing experience that can have a significant impact on an individual's mental and emotional well-being. Trauma can manifest in a variety of ways, including anxiety, depression, post-traumatic stress disorder (PTSD), and other mental health conditions. In this chapter, we will explore the ways in which trauma can affect an individual's career, including how it can impact job performance, relationships with colleagues and managers, and overall job satisfaction.

When an individual experiences trauma, it can affect their ability to focus and concentrate, making it difficult to complete tasks and meet deadlines. This can lead to decreased productivity and job performance, which can ultimately lead to disciplinary action or even termination. Additionally, trauma can cause individuals to struggle with maintaining healthy relationships with colleagues and managers, which can further impact their ability to succeed in their careers.

## 13: TRAUMA AND THE WORKPLACE: HOW TRAUMA CAN AFFECT YOUR CAREER

Trauma can also affect an individual's ability to cope with stress and handle difficult situations in the workplace. For example, an individual who has experienced trauma may struggle with handling criticism from a manager or dealing with a difficult customer. This can lead to increased absenteeism and high turnover rates, which can be detrimental to both the individual and the organization as a whole.

Furthermore, trauma can also affect an individual's ability to advance in their career. Those who have experienced trauma may struggle with networking, public speaking, and other important aspects of career development. This can make it difficult for individuals to secure promotions or move up in their organizations.

However, it is important to note that not all individuals who have experienced trauma will experience these negative effects in the workplace. Many people who have experienced trauma are able to successfully navigate their careers. Additionally, there are resources available to help individuals who are struggling with the effects of trauma in the workplace.

For example, employee assistance programs (EAPs) are

available to provide support and resources to employees who are struggling with mental health issues, including those related to trauma. These programs can provide counseling, therapy, and other forms of support to help employees cope with their experiences and improve their job performance.

Moreover, employers and managers can also play a role in supporting employees who have experienced trauma. This can include providing accommodations such as flexible schedules, additional time off, or changes to job duties. Additionally, managers and colleagues can be trained on how to recognize the signs of trauma and how to provide support to those who are struggling.

In conclusion, trauma can have a significant impact on an individual's career. It can affect job performance, relationships with colleagues and managers, and overall job satisfaction. However, with the right resources and support, individuals who have experienced trauma can successfully navigate their careers. Employers and managers can also play an important role in supporting employees who have experienced trauma and creating a more supportive and understanding work environment.

Another important aspect of addressing trauma in the workplace is creating a culture of openness and understanding. Many individuals who have experienced trauma may feel ashamed or embarrassed to talk about their experiences, which can further exacerbate the negative effects of trauma. By creating a culture where individuals feel safe and supported to talk about their experiences, employers and managers can help to mitigate the negative effects of trauma.

Additionally, employers can also provide training and education on trauma and its effects, for both employees and managers. This can help to increase understanding and awareness of the issue, and promote a more supportive and inclusive workplace.

It's also important to note that some individuals may require accommodations and support in order to function well in their jobs. These accommodations can include flexible work schedules, modified job duties, or additional time off for therapy and treatment. Employers should be willing to work with employees to provide these accommodations, as they can make a significant difference in helping individuals to manage the effects of trauma and be successful in their careers.

In summary, trauma can have a significant impact on an individual's career, but with the right resources and support, individuals can successfully navigate their careers. Employers and managers play an important role in creating a supportive and understanding work environment, and providing resources and support for employees who have experienced trauma. By creating a culture of openness and understanding, providing training and education, and offering accommodations, employers can help to mitigate the negative effects of trauma and promote a more inclusive and supportive workplace.

# 14: Trauma and the Legal System: Navigating the Challenges of Trauma and the Justice System

Trauma and the legal system can be a challenging and difficult topic to navigate. Trauma can affect individuals in a variety of ways and can have a significant impact on their ability to participate in the legal system. This chapter will explore the challenges of trauma and the justice system and provide strategies for navigating these challenges.

Trauma can be defined as a psychological response to a traumatic event or series of events. It can include symptoms such as anxiety, depression, and post-traumatic stress disorder (PTSD). Trauma can also affect an individual's cognitive abilities, including memory, attention, and decision-making. These symptoms can make it difficult for a person to participate in the legal system, particularly if they are a victim or witness in a criminal case.

Victims of trauma may have difficulty remembering details of the traumatic event or may be reluctant to talk about it. This can make it difficult for them to provide testimony in court or for prosecutors to build a strong case. Additionally, trauma can cause anxiety and distress, which can make it difficult for a victim to participate in court proceedings.

Trauma can also affect the way a person perceives and interprets events. This can make it difficult for them to understand legal proceedings and can also affect their ability to make decisions. For example, a victim of trauma may be hesitant to testify in court or may be unsure about whether to press charges against their abuser.

Trauma can also affect an individual's ability to participate in the legal system if they are a defendant in a criminal case. Trauma can affect an individual's decision-making and can also make it difficult for them to understand the legal proceedings. Additionally, trauma can cause anxiety and distress, which can make it difficult for a defendant to participate in court proceedings.

The criminal justice system can be a traumatic experience for victims, witnesses, and defendants. The legal process can be long and drawn out, and individuals may have to relive the traumatic event multiple times. Additionally, the criminal justice system can be a stressful and intimidating experience, particularly for individuals who have experienced trauma.

To navigate the challenges of trauma and the legal system, it is important to understand the impact of trauma and to work with professionals who are trained to support individuals who have experienced trauma. This can include working with therapists, counselors, and other mental health professionals.

Victims and witnesses of trauma may also benefit from advocacy services that provide support and guidance throughout the legal process. These services can help individuals understand the legal proceedings and can also provide emotional support. Additionally, victims and witnesses may benefit from participating in support groups or other forms of peer support.

For defendants who have experienced trauma, it is important to work with attorneys who are familiar with the impact of trauma and who can provide support and guidance throughout the legal process. Additionally, defendants may benefit from working with mental health professionals who can provide support and treatment for trauma.

It is also important for the legal system to take into account the impact of trauma when making decisions about criminal cases. This can include providing accommodations for victims and witnesses who have experienced trauma and taking into account the impact of trauma when determining sentences for defendants.

In conclusion, trauma and the legal system can be a challenging and difficult topic to navigate. Trauma can affect individuals in a variety of ways and can have a significant impact on their ability to participate in the legal system. To navigate these challenges, it is important to understand the impact of trauma and to work with professionals who are trained to support individuals who have experienced trauma. Additionally, it is important for the legal system to take into account the impact of trauma when making decisions about criminal cases.

Another important aspect to consider when navigating the challenges of trauma and the legal system is the role of trauma-informed practice. Trauma-informed practice involves understanding the impact of trauma on individuals and adapting the legal system to better serve those who have experienced trauma. This can include training for legal professionals on the effects of trauma, creating a more welcoming and understanding environment in courtrooms, and using language that is sensitive to the needs of trauma survivors.

Additionally, it is important for legal professionals to understand the intersectionality of trauma. Individuals who have experienced trauma may also have other marginalized identities, such as being a person of color or being a member of the LGBTQ+ community. These identities can compound the effects of trauma and can also affect an individual's experiences within the legal system. Therefore, it is important for legal professionals to be aware of and sensitive to the intersectionality of trauma.

Another key aspect of navigating the challenges of trauma and the legal system is understanding the role of restorative justice. Restorative justice is an approach to justice that focuses on repairing harm caused by crime and working with victims, offenders, and the community to find solutions that are fair and healing. This approach can be particularly beneficial for individuals who have experienced trauma, as it can provide them with a sense of empowerment and agency in the legal process.

In order to effectively navigate the challenges of trauma and the legal system, it is essential for individuals, legal professionals, and the legal system as a whole to work together. This includes understanding the impact of trauma, providing support and accommodations for individuals who have experienced trauma, and implementing trauma-informed practices within the legal system. Only by taking a holistic approach can we truly address the challenges of trauma and the legal system and ensure that justice is served for all.

In conclusion, trauma and the legal system can be a difficult and challenging topic to navigate. Trauma can have a significant impact on an individual's ability to participate in the legal system and can also affect the way in which legal decisions are made. To navigate these challenges, it is important for individuals, legal professionals, and the legal system as a whole to understand the impact of trauma and to implement trauma-informed practices. Additionally, a holistic approach that considers restorative justice and intersectionality of trauma is essential for providing a fair and healing justice system for all.

# 15: Trauma and the Impact on Children and Families

Trauma is an event or series of events that causes significant harm or distress to an individual or group of individuals. The effects of trauma can be long-lasting and have a profound impact on the mental and physical well-being of those affected. Children and families are particularly vulnerable to the effects of trauma, as they are often unable to understand or cope with the traumatic event.

Trauma can take many forms, including physical, emotional, and sexual abuse, neglect, natural disasters, and exposure to violence. Children and families who experience trauma may display a wide range of symptoms, including anxiety, depression, post-traumatic stress disorder (PTSD), and behavioral problems. These symptoms can have a significant impact on a child's ability to form healthy relationships, perform well in school, and function in other areas of life.

Children who have experienced trauma may have difficulty trusting others, feel detached or detached from their emotions, and experience flashbacks or nightmares related to the traumatic event. They may also exhibit aggressive or self-destructive behavior, such as fighting or substance abuse. These symptoms can be difficult to recognize and understand, and can be misinterpreted as disciplinary or behavioral issues rather than symptoms of trauma.

Families who have experienced trauma may also have difficulty functioning as a unit. Parents may struggle with their own mental health issues, including depression and PTSD, and may have difficulty providing the emotional support and stability that their children need. They may also have difficulty communicating with each other or with their children, which can further complicate the healing process.

It's important to recognize that trauma does not discriminate and can happen to anyone, regardless of race, socio-economic status, or other factors. It's also important to note that trauma can have a cumulative effect, meaning that even small traumas can add up over time and have a significant impact on a child's mental and emotional well-being.

Treatment for trauma can take many forms, including therapy, medication, and support groups. It's important to find a treatment that is tailored to the specific needs of the child and family. Trauma-focused cognitive behavioral therapy

(TF-CBT) is a form of therapy that has been shown to be effective in treating children and families who have experienced trauma. TF-CBT is a short-term, structured therapy that focuses on helping children and families understand and process their traumatic experiences, and learn new coping strategies to deal with the symptoms of trauma.

In addition to therapy, medication can also be an effective treatment for trauma-related symptoms, such as anxiety and depression. Medication should always be used in conjunction with therapy and should be prescribed by a qualified mental health professional.

Support groups can also be an important part of the healing process for children and families who have experienced trauma. Support groups provide a safe and supportive environment where children and families can share their experiences, learn from others, and receive support and encouragement.

It's important to remember that healing from trauma is a process and it can take time. Children and families may experience setbacks and may need to revisit certain topics or issues as they continue to heal. It's important to be patient and understanding, and to provide ongoing support and encouragement.

In conclusion, trauma can have a significant and lasting impact on children and families. It's important to recognize the symptoms of trauma and to provide appropriate treatment and support. With the right care and support, children and families can heal and move forward with their lives.

It's also important to remember that trauma does not only affect the individual who experienced it, but it also affects the entire family. Children and families often have to navigate the aftermath of trauma together, and it's essential to provide support and resources to the entire family unit.

Another important aspect of trauma is the recognition of its intergenerational effects. Trauma can be passed down from one generation to another, as parents who have experienced trauma may have difficulty providing a stable and safe environment for their children. This can lead to cycles of trauma and can make it harder for future generations to heal and move on from traumatic experiences.

Additionally, it's essential to understand that trauma can

have different effects on different people, even within the same family. Each person's experience and response to trauma are unique and should be acknowledged and respected.

Prevention is also an important aspect of addressing trauma. It's crucial to educate communities and families about the signs and effects of trauma, as well as providing resources and support to individuals and families who may be at risk of experiencing trauma.

In order to address the impact of trauma on children and families, it's essential to have a comprehensive approach that involves multiple sectors such as healthcare, education, social services, and criminal justice. Collaboration between these sectors is crucial in order to provide the appropriate support and resources for children and families affected by trauma.

In summary, trauma can have a lasting and profound impact on children and families. It's essential to recognize the symptoms of trauma, provide appropriate treatment and support, and address the intergenerational and systemic factors that contribute to the effects of trauma. By providing the necessary resources and support, children and families can heal and move forward with their lives.

# 16: Trauma and Spirituality: How Trauma Can Affect Faith and Beliefs

Trauma and spirituality are often intertwined, as individuals may turn to their faith or beliefs for comfort and understanding during difficult times. However, trauma can also have a profound impact on one's spirituality, potentially leading to feelings of betrayal, abandonment, and loss of meaning.

When an individual experiences trauma, they may question the belief that they previously held in a higher power or the concept of a benevolent universe. They may feel that their faith has been tested and found wanting, leading to feelings of anger and resentment towards their religion or belief system. Trauma can also lead to a loss of trust in the world and in others, making it difficult for an individual to connect with a higher power or find solace in spiritual practices.

Additionally, some individuals may feel that their faith or beliefs were responsible for their trauma, either through the actions of a religious leader or institution, or through the belief that they were being punished for their sins. This can lead to feelings of betrayal and abandonment, and may cause an individual to distance themselves from their faith or beliefs.

On the other hand, some individuals may find that their faith or beliefs provide them with a sense of strength and resilience during times of trauma. They may find comfort in the idea that their suffering has a greater purpose or that they are being tested in order to become a stronger person. They may also find solace in religious or spiritual practices, such as prayer, meditation, or connecting with a community of believers.

However, it's important to note that for some individuals, connecting with their faith or belief system may be challenging, and that's okay. Trauma can change us and our ways of thinking, and it's possible that an individual may find that they no longer identify with the religion or belief system they once held. It's important for individuals to allow themselves the space and time to process their experiences and to find meaning and purpose in their own way.

In summary, trauma can have a significant impact on an individual's spirituality, potentially leading to feelings of betrayal, abandonment, and loss of meaning. However, it's important to remember that different people have different ways of coping with trauma and finding meaning, and that it's important to respect and support an individual's unique journey.

It's also important for individuals who are struggling with the effects of trauma on their spirituality to seek out professional help. A therapist or counselor who is trained in trauma-informed care can provide support and guidance as an individual navigates the complex emotions and beliefs that may arise from their experiences. They can also help an individual develop coping strategies and resilience, and may provide referrals to support groups or other resources that can be beneficial.

Additionally, it can be helpful for individuals to explore other forms of spirituality or religion that may resonate with them more after experiencing trauma. For example, some individuals may find that nature-based spirituality or mindfulness practices provide a sense of peace and connection that traditional religions no longer do. It's important for individuals to explore different paths and find what works best for them.

It's also important to remember that healing from trauma is a process and it doesn't happen overnight. It may take time for an individual to come to terms with the trauma they have experienced and how it has affected their spirituality. It's important to be patient and compassionate with oneself and to take the time needed to heal.

In conclusion, trauma can have a significant impact on an individual's spirituality, but it's important to remember that healing is possible and that different paths may be taken to find meaning and purpose. It's essential to seek professional help, explore different spiritual practices, and be patient with oneself in the healing process. Remember that healing is a journey, not a destination, and that it's important to be gentle with oneself during this time.

# 17: Moving Forward: Finding Purpose and Meaning After Trauma

Trauma can be a devastating and life-altering event. It can leave us feeling lost, confused, and without a sense of purpose or direction. But it is important to remember that healing is possible, and that we can move forward and find meaning and purpose in our lives again.

The first step in moving forward after trauma is to acknowledge and accept that it has happened. Denying or suppressing the trauma will only prolong the healing process. It is important to give yourself time and space to grieve and process the emotions that come with the trauma. This may include seeking support from a therapist or counselor, or joining a support group for people who have experienced similar trauma.

Once you have begun to process the trauma, it is important to focus on self-care. This includes taking care of your physical, emotional, and mental well-being. Eating a healthy diet, getting enough sleep, and regular exercise can all help to promote healing. It is also important to find healthy ways to cope with stress and anxiety, such as through mindfulness practices like meditation or yoga.

## 17: MOVING FORWARD: FINDING PURPOSE AND MEANING AFTER TRAUMA

As you begin to heal, it is also important to find ways to integrate the trauma into your life. This may include finding meaning in the experience, such as by using it to help others who have experienced similar trauma. It may also involve finding a new sense of purpose or direction in life. This may involve returning to school or starting a new career, or simply finding ways to give back to your community.

Another important aspect of moving forward after trauma is to focus on building and maintaining positive relationships. Surrounding yourself with supportive and understanding people can provide much-needed emotional support and encouragement during this difficult time. It is also important to find ways to connect with others who have experienced similar trauma, as this can help to provide a sense of validation and understanding.

As you continue to heal and move forward, it is important to remember that healing is not a linear process. There may be setbacks and triggers that cause the trauma to feel fresh again. It is important to be patient with yourself and to understand that healing takes time. It is also important to remember that it is not necessary to achieve a state of complete healing in order to move forward and find purpose and meaning in life again.

In conclusion, moving forward after trauma can be a difficult and challenging process, but it is possible. By acknowledging and accepting the trauma, focusing on self-care, finding ways to integrate the trauma into your life, building positive relationships, and being patient with yourself, you can begin to heal and find purpose and meaning in your life again. Remember to reach out for help, be kind to yourself and don't give up hope.

It's important to know that healing is a personal journey, what works for one person may not work for another, so be open to explore different options and different paths. It's also important to remind yourself that trauma does not define you and you are capable of overcoming it and finding a new path in life.

Another important aspect of moving forward after trauma is to focus on the present and the future, rather than dwelling on the past. This may involve setting goals for yourself and working towards them, whether they are related to your career, personal relationships, or personal growth. By setting and achieving goals, you can begin to regain a sense of control over your life and a sense of purpose.

It may also be helpful to engage in activities that bring you joy and fulfillment. This can include hobbies, volunteer work, or other interests that you are passionate about. Engaging in activities that you enjoy can help to take your mind off of the trauma and provide a sense of accomplishment and satisfaction.

Another important aspect of moving forward after trauma is to focus on forgiveness. Forgiveness is not about forgetting or excusing the actions of the person or event that caused the trauma, but rather about letting go of the anger and resentment that can hold us back. Forgiving the person or event can help to release the emotional burden and move forward in a positive direction.

In addition, it's important to learn from the trauma and use it as an opportunity for personal growth. Trauma can be a powerful teacher that can help us to develop resilience, empathy, and a deeper understanding of ourselves and others. This can give us a new perspective on life and open up new opportunities for growth and self-discovery.

## 17: MOVING FORWARD: FINDING PURPOSE AND MEANING AFTER TRAUMA

Moving forward after trauma can be a difficult and challenging journey, but it is not impossible. With patience, self-care, and a focus on the present and future, it is possible to heal and find purpose and meaning in life again. Remember to reach out for help, be kind to yourself and don't give up hope.

It's important to remember that healing is not a destination, it's a process, and it's not a one-time event. It's a continuous journey that requires effort and commitment. You may stumble or fall down, but you can always get back up and keep moving forward.

In conclusion, Moving forward after trauma is a process that requires effort and commitment. By acknowledging and accepting the trauma, focusing on self-care, finding ways to integrate the trauma into your life, building positive relationships, setting goals and focusing on the present and future, forgiveness, and learning from the trauma, you can begin to heal and find purpose and meaning in your life again. Remember to reach out for help, be kind to yourself and don't give up hope.

# 18: Conclusion: The Importance of Continuing Support and Self-Discovery in Trauma Recovery

Trauma recovery is a lifelong process that requires ongoing support and self-discovery. The road to healing from trauma can be difficult and bumpy, but with the right support and resources, individuals can learn to manage their symptoms and live fulfilling lives.

The importance of continuing support in trauma recovery cannot be overstated. Trauma survivors often struggle with feelings of isolation and shame, and may not feel comfortable reaching out for help. It is crucial that they have access to a supportive community, whether that be in the form of therapy, support groups, or loved ones. Having a safe space to process and share their experiences can help individuals feel less alone and more understood.

In addition to ongoing support, self-discovery is also crucial in trauma recovery. Trauma can leave individuals feeling disconnected from themselves and their emotions. Through self-discovery, individuals can learn to understand and accept their experiences and emotions, rather than repressing or denying them. This can lead to greater self-awareness and self-compassion, which can help individuals build a more resilient and fulfilling life.

There are many different forms of therapy that can help individuals in their trauma recovery journey. Cognitive Behavioral Therapy (CBT) is one of the most widely-used evidence-based therapies and can help individuals learn to manage their symptoms and improve their overall well-being. Eye Movement Desensitization and Reprocessing (EMDR) is a therapy that can help individuals process traumatic memories and reduce symptoms of trauma such as anxiety, depression, and nightmares. Other therapies such as Mindfulness-Based Stress Reduction (MBSR) and yoga can also be beneficial for trauma recovery.

In addition to traditional therapy, alternative forms of healing such as art therapy, music therapy, and journaling can also be helpful for trauma survivors. These forms of therapy can provide individuals with a creative outlet for expressing their emotions, which can be especially beneficial for those who may not feel comfortable verbalizing their experiences.

## 18: CONCLUSION: THE IMPORTANCE OF CONTINUING SUPPORT AND SELF-DISCOVERY IN TRAUMA RECOVERY

It is important to note that trauma recovery is not always linear and individuals may experience setbacks. It is important to understand that healing is a process and it can take time. It is also important to note that everyone is different and there is no "one size fits all" approach to trauma recovery. Some individuals may find that traditional therapy works best for them, while others may find that alternative forms of healing are more beneficial.

In conclusion, trauma recovery is a lifelong process that requires ongoing support and self-discovery. Having access to a supportive community and various forms of therapy can help individuals manage their symptoms and improve their overall well-being. Remember that healing is a process and everyone is different, so it is important to find what works best for you.

It is also important for individuals to understand that healing from trauma is not just about managing symptoms, but also about learning to live a fulfilling life. This can involve setting and achieving personal goals, building healthy relationships, and finding a sense of purpose. Trauma recovery can also involve learning to accept and forgive oneself for past experiences and mistakes, as well as learning to let go of negative thoughts and beliefs about oneself.

For some individuals, trauma recovery may also involve facing and addressing the root cause of their trauma. This may involve seeking justice for past injustices, such as filing a report or pressing charges against an abuser. It may also involve addressing systemic issues, such as advocating for policy changes or participating in activism.

It is also important to understand that trauma recovery is not just the responsibility of the individual. As a society, we must work to create a culture of understanding and support for trauma survivors. This includes educating ourselves about the effects of trauma, being aware of the signs of trauma in others, and being willing to offer help and support when needed. It also includes working to eliminate the root causes of trauma, such as poverty, racism, and discrimination.

In conclusion, trauma recovery is a lifelong process that requires ongoing support, self-discovery, and a commitment to living a fulfilling life. It is important to understand that

## 18: CONCLUSION: THE IMPORTANCE OF CONTINUING SUPPORT AND SELF-DISCOVERY IN TRAUMA RECOVERY

everyone's journey is unique, and it is essential to find the right forms of therapy and support that work best for the individual. As a society, we must also strive to create a culture of understanding and support for trauma survivors, and work towards eliminating the root causes of trauma. Remember that healing is possible and with the right support, individuals can learn to manage their symptoms, and live fulfilling lives.

# Thank You

As we reach the end of this book, I want to say thanks for reading this book.

I want to get this information out to as many people as possible. If you found this book helpful, I would greatly appreciate you leaving me a review. This helps others find the book as well.

# Disclaimer

This document is geared towards providing exact and reliable information in regards to the topic and issue covered. The publication is sold on the idea that the publisher is not required to render an accounting, officially permitted, or otherwise, qualified services. If advice is necessary, legal, financial, medical or professional, a practiced individual in the profession should be ordered.

This information is not presented by a financial or medical practitioner and is for entertainment, educational and informational purposes only. The content is not intended as a substitute for professional medical advice, diagnosis, or treatment. Always seek the advice of your physician or other qualified health care provider with any questions you may have regarding a medical condition. Never disregard professional medical advice or delay in seeking it because of something you have read.

The information provided herein is stated to be truthful and consistent, in that any liability, in terms of inattention or otherwise, by any usage or abuse of any policies, processes, or directions contained within is the solitary and utter responsibility of the recipient reader. Under no circumstances

# DISCLAIMER

will any legal responsibility or blame be held against the publisher for any reparation, damages, or monetary loss due to the information herein, either directly or indirectly.